Experiential Perspectives of Teachers in an Inclusive Classroom

DR. EVELYN IFY NWADINOBI

Experiential Perspectives of Teachers in an Inclusive Classroom

Copyright © 2018 by **Dr. Evelyn Ify Nwadinobi**
ISBN: 978-1-944652-61-6

Printed in the United States of America. All rights reserved solely by the publisher. This book or parts thereof may not be reproduced in any form, stored in a retrieval system, or transmitted in any form by any means - electronic, mechanical, photocopy.

Published By:
Cornerstone Publishing
A division of Cornerstone Creativity Group LLC
+1 516-547-4999   Info@thecornerstonepublishers.com
www.thecornerstonepublishers.com

Author's Information

For speaking engagement, training consulting or to order books by Dr. Evelyn Ify Nwadinobi

Please call +1 248-943-0127 or

send email to: e_nwadinobi@yahoo.com

DEDICATION

I dedicate this dissertation to my amazing family. To my biggest supporters – John K, Ogechi, Dike, Ezinne and Chisom – thank you for being there every step of the way.

To my late brother, Dr. Kevin Uwazurike, the Ebubedike 1 and the Ekwueme 1 of Umunnakanu Owerre ancient Kingdom in Ehime Mbano local Government. I know that l have made you proud. ENYINNAYA UWAZURIKE, the grandfather of inclusivity. Thank you for your constant encouragement.

ACKNOWLEDGMENTS

I would like to acknowledge my advisor, Dr. Brandy Kamm, for her tireless input and support on this project. I could not have done this without your help. To my committee members, Drs. Janice Powell and Brian Creasman, your feedback has helped shape this dissertation into a project of which I am immensely proud. Thank you.

ABSTRACT

Inclusive educational settings have become the norm as schools aim to educate disabled students in environments least restrictive to their development (U.S. Department of Education, 2004). This study was conducted in order to assess teacher perceptions of inclusion academically, socially, and behaviorally for general and special education students. Informed by sociocultural theory (Vygotsky, 1978), and integrated threat theory (Bustillos & Silvan-Ferrero, 2013), this research aimed to give voice to those most instrumental in implementing inclusion successfully and effectively. Utilizing open-ended interviews and qualitative analyses coded by Excel and NVivo software, the study discovered that teacher participants perceived the main benefit of inclusion to be the provision of leadership training and sensitivity for general education students and feelings of acceptance amongst special education students. However, teachers reported that the negative impacts of inclusion include more frequent incidents of disruptive behavior causing distraction from learning as well as more stringent academic standards and increased instances of bullying for the special education students. Key suggestions provided by participants included a need for additional training for teachers on co-teaching methods and special education student sensitivity. The participants also reported the necessity of smaller class sizes and a desire to return to the traditional classroom environment. This study benefits the educational community by revealing the necessity of special-education training workshops and support personnel to ease the integration of inclusive classrooms for both students and teachers. Implementation of such policy changes will make the perceptions of educators tangible.

Keywords: inclusion, general education, special education, disability, achievement, bullying

CONTENTS

DEDICATION..5

ACKNOWLEDGMENTS..6

ABSTRACT..7

INTRODUCTION..13

Background, Context, History, and Conceptual Framework for the Problem......................................14

Statement of the Problem...15

Purpose of the Study..17

Research Questions..23

Rationale, Relevance, and Significance of the Study...24

Definition of Terms...25

Assumptions, Delimitations, and Limitations..........29

Summary 31

LITERATURE REVIEW 33
Change and Challenges..............................38
Conceptual Framework..............................40
Review of Research Literature 44
Review of Methodological Issues and Literature.....48
Synthesis of Research Findings..............................51
Perspectives of Teachers..............................52
The Impact of Labeling..............................57
Impact of Bullying..............................59
Critique of Previous Research on Classroom Inclusiveness..............................62
Summary..............................66

METHODOLOGY..............................71
Research Questions..............................73
Purpose and Rationale of the Study..............................74
Methodological Design..............................76
Methodological Challenges..............................80
Sample Population Specific/Population General..............................85
Research Instrument..............................87
Research Procedures..............................88

Data Analysis..88
Limitations of the Research Design......................90
Expected Findings...94
Conflict of Interest Assessment............................95
Researcher's Position..96
Ethical Issues in the Study..97
Summary..99

DATA ANALYSIS AND RESULTS...............101
Descriptive Data..103
Data Collection Procedure..................................104
Data Analysis and Procedures...........................104
Responses to Research..110
Responses to Research Question 2...............121
Summary..132

SUMMARY, CONCLUSIONS, AND RECOM MENDATIONS...135
Summary and Discussion of Results in Relation to the Literature..136
Limitations..146
Implications of the Results for Practice, Policy, and Theory..147

Recommendations for Further Research............151
Conclusion..152
References..154

Chapter 1
Introduction to the Problem

Inclusive classrooms have become the norm for many learning-disabled students (U.S. Department of Education, 1992). In the inclusive classroom setting, schools place learning- disabled students in the same classroom with non-learning-disabled students. Students are taught the same curriculum. Regardless of the severity of the learning disability, schools place the student in the least restrictive environment (U.S. Department of Education, 2004). Teacher attitudes toward inclusion are important to the success of students in the inclusive environment whether learning-disabled or in the general student population. This research explored teachers' perspectives of inclusive classroom environments on learning-disabled and non- learning-disabled high school seniors in central Michigan.

BACKGROUND, CONTEXT, HISTORY, AND CONCEPTUAL FRAMEWORK FOR THE PROBLEM

Since 2000 in the United States, policies were shifted toward the inclusive classroom as standard for all students (Dudley-Marling & Burns, 2014). Within these classrooms, teachers create an inclusive classroom environment. The teacher is responsible for ensuring students grasp the subjects and progress toward their academic goals. Teachers can develop unfavorable attitudes toward students who are not meeting academic expectations. Vaz, Wilson, Falkmer, Sim, Scott, and Cordier (2015) found teacher attitudes toward inclusion are not based on a specific ideology or theory, but rather on personal experiences in the classroom. This suggests that teachers' previous experiences with inclusion affected teachers' attitudes toward learning-disabled students in their inclusive classrooms settings. Vaz et al. (2015) suggested that the ideology behind inclusion was less relevant than the real world, lived experiences of teachers, the inclusive classroom and its effects on both learning-disabled and non-learning-disabled students.

Sometimes teachers struggle to create a positive atmosphere in inclusive classrooms. Cameroon (2014) found that teachers in the general classroom setting have difficulty balancing time between providing for special needs students who require extra attention while still attending to the needs of the other students. For the learning-disabled student, inclusion can lead to a negative academic classroom experience. Teacher perceptions of the student can add to their negative experience. They may experience social struggles, such as bullying, rejection, and difficulty in developing close relationships with peers, which can lead to low self-esteem, low academic performance, anxiety, and depression (Wiener, 2014). Conversely, if the student is placed in a classroom where the teacher has a positive perception toward inclusion, it can produce positive outcomes for the learning-disabled student. These positive outcomes can include improved self-esteem, a feeling of belonging socially, and improved academic performance.

STATEMENT OF THE PROBLEM

The focus of this dissertation was to explore teachers' perspectives of inclusive classroom environments for learning-disabled and non-learning-disabled high school seniors in select central Michigan high schools. Vorhaus (2014) asserted that respect is owed to all persons, including persons with learning difficulties and disabilities. He identified characteristics of successful teaching and learning environments. These included treating the profoundly disabled learner as a person, insistence on individualized learning, and the ability to establish a close relationship between teaching and caring for the vulnerable learner. Vorhaus (2014) supported this view with detailed testimonies from individuals with disabilities on their social and learning experiences inside and outside the classroom, effectively revealing how integral a role teachers play in their learning trajectories.

Numerous studies show how inclusive instructional strategies used with learning-disabled students in general classrooms improved academic status (Beauchamp-Pryor, 2013; Hehir & Katzman, 2013; Henninger & Gupta, 2014; Idol, 2006). Additionally, the inclusion of learning-disabled students in general classrooms can defuse the opinions of other students that learning-disabled students are different (Yell, Conroy, Katsiyannis, & Conroy, 2013). Inclusion provides benefits to all students (Beauchamp-Pryor, 2013). This can affect teacher perceptions of the inclusion classroom in a positive manner. However, Cameroon (2014) and Wiener (2014) found that inclusion leads to negative classroom experiences due to social struggles or lack of sufficient attention from teachers. This can lead to negative perceptions of learning disabled students by the teachers.

Vaz et al. (2015) found that teacher attitudes can have an impact on academic achievement. Some teachers harbor negative perspectives about special-needs students and their ability to learn. This has negative consequences on the experiences of special-needs students. Through this qualitative study, this researcher explored teachers' perspectives of inclusive classroom environments for learning-disabled and non-learning-disabled students in central Michigan high schools.

PURPOSE OF THE STUDY

Qualitative research methodology was utilized to explore teachers' perspectives of inclusive classroom settings for high school seniors' learning-disabled and non-learning-disabled students in participating Michigan high schools. It gained the perspective of teachers on how learning-disabled students are treated by other students. In addition, by allowing teachers to understand how their perceptions affect the learning environment, they may be able to improve the social environment, which may benefit students' learning processes. Exploring the experiences of the teachers may provide valuable insight into teacher attitudes and classroom design. This additional insight could help improve future outcomes for all students.

Williams, Pazey, Shelby, and Yates (2013) established that learning-disabled students are exposed more frequently to exclusionary discipline than non-learning-disabled students. Integrated threat theory (Bustillos & Silvan-Ferrero, 2013) approach was used to discover perceived threats from the perspectives of school administrators. This was particularly the case regarding administrators' concerns over their values, individual job performance beliefs, and maintaining necessary resources for both themselves and their schools. Integrated threat theory attempts to explain the existence of perceived threats between different social groups (Bustillos & Silvan-Ferrero, 2013). The two most common perceived threats are physical harm and loss of financial resources. Special education teachers expressed feeling threatened when presented with the challenges of numerous types of learning disabilities, as well as how different schools view children with learning disabilities. Integrated threat theory of prejudice asserts that threat causes negative attitudes toward a group and supposes that such threats may come from different sources (Bustillos & Silvan-Ferrero, 2013). Bustillos and Silvan-Ferrero (2013) found that perceived threats for resources and intergroup anxiety were effective mediators in the process of group conflict, while social dominance orientation was a strong predictor of attitudes toward people who were physically disabled. While these social psychological theories provide significant context for the existence of negative attitudes toward individuals with learning disabilities, it is necessary to explore teacher's perspectives of inclusive classroom environments for learning-disabled and non-learning-disabled high school seniors in select high schools in central Michigan.

In the United States, and internationally, school systems are moving away from isolating and excluding people with disabilities from mainstream education. This may be due to the requirement to provide education in the least restrictive environment. Countries across the world are establishing disability policies that substantially protect and guarantee equal rights to all citizens (Mariga & McConkey, 2014). Inclusive classrooms are becoming an increasing priority in school systems in developed countries (Tkachyk, 2013). The equalization of opportunities requires new processes to deliver the goals of the rights of people with disabilities to remain in their communities while receiving schooling and necessary social support within the usual available structures (Tkachyk, 2013). School systems and societies are changing their outlooks on the fate of learning-disabled students (Beauchhamp-Pryor, 2013), although some research questioned the trend of the inclusive classroom and its merit (Tkachyk, 2013).

Schools embrace inclusive classrooms because of the benefits children with disabilities gain from the inclusion setting (Henninger & Gupta, 2014). Among these benefits is the ability to interact with peers and gain social skills. Learning-disabled students have an inherent right to receive their education in the environment least restrictive to their educational growth. In the inclusive classroom, learning-disabled students gain the benefit of imitation, emulating peer behaviors. Higher expectations in inclusive classrooms cause students with disabilities to be challenged, gain confidence, and develop stronger self-images (Henninger & Gupta, 2014). Similarly, Kioko and Makoelle (2014) suggested that including learning-disabled students in general education, instead of separating or isolating them, engenders survival instincts in the students. Learning-disabled students participate in class with non-learning-disabled students, and by so doing, learn how to compete and challenge themselves (Kioko & Makoelle, 2014).

Including learning-disabled students in the inclusive classroom also benefits the other students by exposing them to students with different academic abilities (Henninger &Gupta, 2014). According to Kioko and Makoelle (2014), disability is a social construct that compels recognition of the challenges that exists within a social stratum. Inclusion helps all students become more understanding and empathetic toward others. One advantage is that inclusion helps normally developing students maintain positive attitudes toward diverse groups of people (Henninger & Gupta, 2014). However, one could consider the opposite true that valuable instructional time could be taken away from typically developing students in order to provide for the needs of the disabled students.

Parents advocate for inclusive education. Parental involvement is an important factor in the development of inclusive education on a global basis. In South Africa, parents advocated for inclusive education in the 1990s and parents became involved in the decision-making processes regarding school placement of their disabled children (Walton, 2011), which led to benefits that included individual rights, equity, and freedom of choice in the implementation of inclusive education programs. In addition to legislation and parental desires, the success of inclusive educational practices depends on the development of collaboration and trust among teachers, parents, and professionals (Walton, 2011). This cooperative environment will allow the child to have greater consistency when transitioning between these environments.

Parents of all students see inclusive settings as the key to the realization of their vision for their children. Parents of gifted students and honors students will benefit by the ability to expose their children to different types of people. They socially interact with many different types of people. They will also benefit through the development of leadership skills by helping disabled students with their academic studies and by providing a social role model. Students, irrespective of their abilities, tend to develop positive understandings of themselves and others in inclusive settings (Alquraini & Gut, 2012). Classroom diversity is enriching because it exposes students to peers who are differently abled, and teaches them to behave socially in a diverse cultural environment (Alquraini & Gut, 2012). Similarities and differences of people in an inclusive classroom setting mimic those that exist in the real world. Inclusive classrooms foster friendship, enable students to confront challenges both socially and academically, and empower students to feel that they are a part of society (Alquraini & Gut, 2012). Since the philosophy of inclusiveness in education seeks to help all children to learn, everyone in the classroom benefits (Alquraini & Gut, 2012). In a nurturing environment, students learn in their own unique styles and at their own pace.

Research enumerates the benefits of inclusiveness of students – disabled and non-disabled – in general classroom settings. While recognizing the societal benefits of inclusion, teachers and parents question if the implementation of full inclusion comes at the expense of the learners' individual needs (Tkachyk, 2013). Educators and school administrators seem to continue to prioritize the needs of learning-disabled students during curricular planning, justifying Tkachyk's (2013) reasoning that modeling an inclusive society should not mean inclusion at all costs. Tkachyk suggested that educators consider what is best for each student and recognized that one size will never fit all. Hehir and Katzman (2013) found that the success of inclusive schools depends largely on the ability of school curriculum to "link to and bolster general education instruction" (p. 274). This means delivering the curriculum in a way that appeals to different types of learners in the classroom.

RESEARCH QUESTIONS

This qualitative research study examined the perspectives of teachers regarding social and academic outcomes for learning-disabled students and non-learning-disabled students in inclusive classroom settings. The following research questions provided the central focus for the research study.

What are perspectives of teachers regarding the inclusive classroom setting and the impact on regular education students, socially, behaviorally, and academically?

What are perspectives of teachers regarding the

inclusive classroom setting and the impact on special education students, socially, behaviorally, and academically?

RATIONALE, RELEVANCE, AND SIGNIFICANCE OF THE STUDY

This study will provide information for teachers, administrators, parents, and students regarding teachers' perspectives on the appropriateness of the inclusive classroom for the learning-disabled student population. It will also provide insight regarding the effects of placement in an inclusive classroom on learning-disabled students. Additionally, it will provide information about the attitudes of teachers in inclusive classrooms, which may provide a better understanding of how theories regarding the inclusive classroom translate to the real world, lived experiences of teachers.

The population included both regular classroom and special education teachers of high school seniors' learning-disabled and non-learning-disabled students in select central Michigan high schools. The researcher conducted this study using structured interview techniques to allow teachers the ability to reflect on their perspectives of the current and future states of learning-disabled (LD) students' academic goals and prospects. The teachers were expected to give complete and detailed answers. This interview method of open-ended questions allowed for in-depth answers that provided great insight. The researcher then transcribed the interview recordings and analyzed the interview responses thematically using narrative coding for content, according to the techniques outlined by Hycner (1985).

Through this study, the researcher explored teachers' perspectives of inclusive classroom environments for high school seniors' learning-disabled and non-learning-disabled students in three central Michigan high schools. This study may assist teachers, administrators, and parents in making better decisions about individual students and developing policies that provide better outcomes for the student population. The overall impact of this study will contribute to the understanding of teacher perspectives and attitudes toward the inclusive classroom, providing a starting point for potential interventions to improve academic outcomes.

DEFINITION OF TERMS

Certain words or phrases in the research study may have different connotative meanings when used in different contexts. In order to clarify the definitions of key words in this study, the researcher utilized the following operational definitions throughout the study.

Children with disabilities. Children with disabilities are those who meet the classification criteria for being in need of special education and related services as defined by federal law (Alquraini & Gut, 2012).

Full inclusion. Full inclusion is a type of inclusive environment in which schools place students in inclusive classrooms without regard to any condition or handicap (Avissar, Lict, & Vogel, 2016).

General education. General education is content-driven instruction that is in accordance with state requirements and needs of students in helping them to pass proficiency tests. This content is provided to all students and does not address the needs of individuals (Avissar et al., 2016).

Inclusion - Inclusion refers to the placement of all students, including those with learning disabilities in the general classroom, to be educated together for the majority of their school day (Michailakis & Reich, 2009).

Individualized education program (IEP) - The IEP is a written plan provided for every special-needs student. It outlines the expectations and individual plan for achieving goals in the academic setting. The student's individual progress is measured against the standard (Hehir & Katzman, 2013).

Learning disability. A learning disability is a clinical disorder that affects one or more basic physical or psychological functions that are important to understanding or using spoken and written language (Woodcock & Vialle, 2010). It can affect the ability to think, listen, speak, write, read, spell, or perform mathematical operations. It also includes any condition that affects perceptual capabilities, such as dyslexia, minimal brain dysfunction, injury to the brain or nervous system, or developmental aphasia (Woodcock & Vialle, 2010).

Least restrictive environment (LRE) - The least restrictive environment refers to the mandates that every special needs student has the right to receive an education that provides the least restriction to their academic and social development as determined by their individualized education program (Hulgin & Drake, 2011).

Public Law (PL) 94–142 - The Education for All Handicapped Children Act. This act defines and promotes the inclusive setting for learning-disabled students. It serves as a guideline for determining the appropriate academic setting for each student with disabilities.

Related Services - Related services refer to services that are adjunct to the classroom setting, such as transportation, and supportive services such as psychological services, speech pathology, physical therapy, audiology, social work services, therapeutic recreation services, and other services that are needed for student success (Peacock Hill Working Group, 2017).

School System - A school system is defined as a group of schools that are responsible for providing educational services in a certain geographic area of the United States (MacFarlane & Woolfson, 2013).

Special Education - Special education is an educational program designed to meet the needs of learning-disabled students that is conducted under the direction of a teacher who is certified for the provision of such services to the special needs population (Katsiyannis, Yell, & Bradley, 2001).

Specific Learning Disability - Specific Learning Disability comprises a disorder that involves one or more of the basic psychological processes which are involved in understanding or using language that manifests itself in the imperfect ability to listen, think, speak, read, write, spell, or do mathematical calculations (Thornton, McKissick, Spooner, Lo, & Anderson, 2015). It includes conditions such as brain injury, perceptual disabilities, dyslexia, minimal brain dysfunction, or developmental aphasia (Woodcock & Vialle, 2010).

Support Staff - Support staff includes staff other than the special education teacher who provides supervision or adjunct services to assist in the educational process and residential care of special-needs students (Kioko & Makoelle, 2014).

ASSUMPTIONS, DELIMITATIONS, AND LIMITATIONS

Two assumptions were relevant to this study: (a) all the participating teachers would be truthful in their responses on their perceptions regarding how the inclusive classroom affects students, socially, behaviorally, and academically; and (b) the data collected would provide a clear description on how teacher perceptions affect high school seniors' learning-disabled students in inclusive settings. Limitations are uncontrollable factors that threaten the internal validity or credibility of a study. For this study, the limitations included the likelihood that pre- existing attitudes and beliefs might have had an effect on the outcome of the study (Ellis & Levy, 2009; Vaz et al., 2015). Pre-existing teacher attitudes toward learning-disabled students could hinder the study. In addition, teachers of inclusive classrooms may have developed accepting attitudes of learning-disabled students in the classroom. Transferability, defined as the extent to which a study's findings would be applicable and effective in different settings, was of particular relevance to this study (Burchett, Mayhew, Lavis, & Dobrow, 2012). The results of this investigation might be transferable only to populations that are similar to the one used in the study. In addition, the sample population might mean that teachers felt the need to modify their responses for fear of repercussions. This could have significantly affected the conclusions of the research study. It was also possible that the sample population could have been reduced further due to respondents who did not participate.

Relevant delimitations—variables that define the boundaries and limit the generalizability of the study—stem from the demographics of the school system under study (Ellis & Levy, 2009). The particular geographic region and study site might have an impact on the ability to apply the results to other school settings. The results from this study may only apply to the geographic region in which the researcher conducted the study. Schools located in different parts of the country may not have similar characteristics, which may affect results of similar studies. Additionally, other characteristics, such as school size, student, and teacher demographics, may affect the outcomes of the schools' inclusive environments. Therefore, results can only be applied to schools that are similar to the one used in this study.

SUMMARY

This research explored the lived experiences of teachers in inclusive classrooms. The research questions reflected a need to learn more about the teacher perspectives gained from working in inclusive classrooms on how inclusion affects students academically, socially, and behaviorally among general student populations and special-needs students. The results of the study were limited to other school systems that are similar to the school system used in this research. Subsequent chapters explore the literature supporting this research study, research methodology, findings of the study, and a discussion of the results as they apply to the future of the inclusive classroom in The Essence Educational Academy Schools, which is the pseudonym the researcher will be using to refer to the research site in this study.

Chapter 2
Literature Review

In this study, the researcher explored teachers' perspectives of the present and future states of inclusiveness of learning-disabled (LD) students in their educational pursuits, as well as the on-going public and private debates regarding various methods of addressing learning- disabled students' needs. Chen and Chan (2014) described learning disabilities as a number of disorders that affect the way people acquire, retain, organize, and understand information. This study examined critical strategies that can improve learning-disabled (LD) students' educational and social well-being. The purpose of this study was to examine how teacher perspectives in high school seniors' inclusive classroom settings in central Michigan affect both learning disabled and non-learning disabled students socially, behaviorally, and academically.

In examining learning-disabled students in the 21st century, it is important to understand historical trends in the treatment and experience of learning-disabled students in United States school systems. In the mid-twentieth century, people considered learning-disabled students as less than human, refused their entry into schools where non-learning-disabled students attended, and did not admit them at social gatherings (Beauchamp-Pryor, 2013). Discrimination against special-needs students in K-12 education from 1945 to 1965 was both legally permissible and widespread (Eckes & Gibbs, 2012). This phenomenon extended from the student body into the hiring of faculty and staff with disabilities in American schools.

Even when schools did admit learning-disabled students, discrimination within school systems continued. Through the mid-twentieth century, some learning-disabled students were denied, rejected, cursed, discriminated against, and excluded from main school social activities and academic instructions (Middleton, 2009). Additionally, Williams et al. (2013) discovered that learning-disabled students were disproportionately subjected to exclusionary discipline in the school district because of school administrators' perceptions of learning-disabled students. Using Threat Theory, Williams et al. (2013) also found that school administrators revealed negative perceptions of the experiences of learning-disabled students as they relate to their values, beliefs, job performance, and available resources for themselves and their school communities. In response, Williams et al. (2013) recommended effective intervention strategies to alleviate the negative perceptions and to expand administrators' knowledge of diverse students, specifically of learning-disabled students. If school administrators know and understand their learning-disabled students, their innate fears about such students may disappear, creating room for improved working relationships and thereby enabling the administrators to effectively address students' concerns (Williams et al., 2013).

Similarly, Cook and Cameron (2010) described the disparities between school experiences and educational outcomes of learning-disabled students and their class peers. Cook and Cameron identified prejudice and discrimination that existed because teachers and schools discriminated against learning-disabled students through the mid-twentieth century. For instance, they were not permitted to participate in the regular classroom, even if they were capable of doing so with assistance. To address this issue, schools made concerted efforts to teach administrators about the diversities of learning-disabled students. Beauchamp-Pryor (2013) suggested that administrators and teachers should develop skills to meet the needs and concerns of learning-disabled students. Though Williams et al.

(2013) and Beauchamp-Pryor (2013) focused primarily on ways by which teacher and administrator attitudes caused greater exclusionary practices toward students with disabilities; the issue of how such attitudes affect the social and academic behavior of students was not addressed in these studies.

Despite decades of equality legislation, workplace discrimination based on "sex, race, disability, age, sexual orientation, religion or belief, and gender reassignment" continues to prevail in our society (Wright & Conley, 2011, p. 32). However, there seems to be a change in how society perceives people with disabilities. History is inundated with discrimination, incrimination, and rejection of individuals with disabilities (Beauchamp-Pryor, 2013). In the 1960s, there were no formal laws or government services that recognized or protected the needs of learning-disabled students. Since then, attitudes regarding special education have changed. By 1966, Congress established guidelines under Title VI of the Elementary and Secondary Schools Act for the Education of the Handicapped (Yettick, Baker, Wickersham, & Hupfeld, 2014). In 1975, the Public Law 94–142, known as the Education of all Handicapped Children Act, followed. This required that school districts educate children with disabilities in the least restrictive environments (Keogh, 2007). A seminal law that enriched and improved educational opportunities for learning-disabled students in the United States – the Individuals with Disabilities Education Act (IDEA) of 2004 – compelled learning-disabled students to participate in the general education curriculum (Schalock et al., 2010). While the law empowered parents of disabled children in public school to be more proactive in intervening in all aspects of the decision-making that involved their children in special education, it was important to recognize the unexpected effects of inclusion on the parents and families of learning-disabled students (Gasteiger-Klicpera, Klicpera, Gebhardtand, & Schwab, 2013). Obiakor, Harris, Mutua, Rotatori, and Algozzine (2012) advocated for the provision of access to the general education curriculum as required by the No Child Left Behind Act and the Individuals with Disabilities Education Act and recommended practical, disability-related solutions for effectively differentiating instructions in inclusive classrooms.

This literature review includes a brief discussion of the multitude of problems that learning-disabled students face today, the environments in which they learn, the implications of inclusive classrooms for both the learning-disabled and non-learning-disabled students, and a brief discussion of the research on the benefits of inclusive classrooms that equally accommodate all students.

Inclusiveness of students with learning disabilities in mainstream classrooms is comparatively recent in the history of special education (Smith, Polloway, Patton, Dowdy, & Doughty, 2015). Inclusiveness includes academic opportunities, socialization, and the chance to participate in the community through school activities. The recognition of the right of all individuals to participate in community membership is one of the major motives for inclusion. Nonetheless, barriers still exist that prevent the inclusion of students with severe disabilities. Anderson (2012) identified that challenging behavior is a potential barrier to successful inclusion programs, and suggested the development of new approaches to enable both class and specialist teachers to minimize the occurrence of such behavior. Challenging behavior includes aggression, disturbance of other students, refusal to participate, or any other behavior that disrupts students' ability to learn and function in the classroom. Understanding of inclusion will help to improve the future of learning-disabled students in Michigan high schools and beyond.

CHANGE AND CHALLENGES

There remains a mixture of social benefits, costs, concerns, and fear concerning inclusive education. Learning-disabled students are pulled in different emotional directions, between acceptance and rejection, inclusion and exclusion. These dilemmas have led governments, institutions, and education leaderships to embark on the implementation of curricular changes that accommodate the needs of learning-disabled students (Cook & Cameron, 2010). Cook and Cameron (2010) suggested that the state interventions serve to advance the pursuit of technical solutions and social inclusion of disabled persons as a moral rather than a political solution. These interventions urge school systems to support the challenges of students with learning disabilities as well as engage in addressing their problems.

Disability concerns are not exclusive to K-12 education; these concerns extend and are felt at all educational levels. Disabled Students' Programs (DSPs) are one solution in higher education that ensures all students have equal access to educational opportunities that will enable them to reach their highest potential. Through such programs, colleges and universities empower their students to participate freely and actively in all facets of university life (Summer, 2011). Such programs cater to all disabled students, including mobility, visual, hearing or speech impairments, chronic illnesses, head injuries, painful conditions, psychological disabilities, attention deficit disorders, and learning disabilities. The recognition and acceptance of the needs of disabled students compel educational institutions of state and national policies to consider learning disabilities at every level (Summer, 2011).

CONCEPTUAL FRAMEWORK

Vygotsky's sociocultural theory formed the conceptual framework for this study. Lev Vygotsky was a contemporary of Skinner and Piaget (Cherry, 2016). Where Skinner and Piaget emphasized the internal processes involved in learning, Vygotsky (1978) emphasized the child's sociocultural environment. According to Vygotsky's theory, the child's ability to learn is influenced by those around them such as parents, teachers, peers, and the culture in which they live. Vygotsky considered the child's sphere of influence plays a key role in the child's ability to learn. This was especially true for higher-level concepts such as logic, attention, conceptual learning, and the ability to form relationships with others (Cherry, 2016).

Lev Vygotsky believed that all children are born with certain biological constraints on their mind that affect the ability of the child to learn and adapt to their environment. They gain the tools that they need to adapt to these constraints from their culture and social cues. These tools might include note taking and rote memorization. Each culture has its own way of teaching children to learn (Roth & Lee, 2007).

Sociocultural theory suggests that the mechanism for cognitive development is not as universal and uniform as Piaget believed (Vygotsky, 1978). When one applies sociocultural theory to this research study, the perceptions of teachers are in the social and cultural influence of both learning disabled and non-learning disabled students. Teachers' perceptions of the students in the inclusive classroom influence the learning style of the student. This can impact the students' ability to learn.

Experience and personal conversations with high school special education teachers in a Michigan school system revealed how learning-disabled students and their parents struggle with academic and social challenges. Complaints and frustrations abound in school buildings as teachers, administrators, learning-disabled students, and their parents struggle to find solutions (Ong-Dean, 2009). Ridnouer (2011) found an atmosphere of confusion surrounding special education that affects parents, teachers, and students. Ridnouer (2011) suggested that in some cases, special education is still used as a "dumping ground" where schools unload problem students. In others, it provides access to services and accommodations that improve the chances of academic success of children with disabilities. Karande and Kuril (2011) conducted a study involving 12-year-olds with specific learning disabilities, in which parents sought different strategies that enabled them to communicate more effectively and collaborate with schools to provide more effective services for their children with disabilities. This study tied into Vygotsky's (1978) sociocultural theory and emphasized the role of the child's social sphere of influence on learning outcomes through developing a cooperative learning environment that is fundamental in the development of intelligence.

Even now, with inclusive education, learning-disabled students experience discrimination and rejection. Often, the suffering that learning-disabled students experience not only comes from outsiders but also from parents, family members, and teachers (Brown, 2012). Karande and Kuril (2011) found that parents of children with specific learning disability (SpLD) undergo stress in coping with their children's condition. Such family conditions were debilitating in the past when there was no help or support to the families with such difficulties. Fortunately, things are changing as school systems are urged by the federal government to support learning-disabled students and their families. Karande and Kuril (2011) recommended that concerted efforts be made to reduce the unpleasant experiences of students with SpLD during their schooling years to curtail the stress and humiliation that is exerted on their families. Schools can utilize information from research studies to understand the strengths and weaknesses of the family support system. This can assist in the development of a learning plan that is suited to the student's individual needs (Bauer, Wistow, Dixon, & Knapp, 2015).

Learning-disabled students also need protection from bullying and damaging social interactions with classmates and acceptance in their classroom environments so that they do not experience physical or emotional harm from the other students. Cook and Cameron (2010) found a worrisome trend; students in all disability categories receive significantly higher concern and rejection ratings than non-learning-disabled students. Rejection ratings reflect the level of feelings of rejection by their peers. Students with learning disabilities and other behavioral disorders received significantly higher rejection ratings than non-learning-disabled students, and students with behavioral disorders received significantly higher rejection ratings than students' with cognitive disabilities.

With inclusive education also comes the issue of ensuring that teachers have sufficient training and knowledge regarding disabilities and best practices for curriculum. Various studies (Beauchamp-Pryor, 2013; Ong-Dean, 2009; Ridnouer, 2011) evaluated the impact of schooling experience on adolescents with specific learning disability (SpLD) and the need for improving the knowledge of SpLDs of classroom teachers, peers, classmates, and family members. Woodcock and Vialle (2010) showed that increasingly, students with learning disabilities were being educated in the general education setting by general education teachers, creating the need for appropriately trained general education teachers and administrators who use instructional practices that benefit all students. Others have confirmed this claim as they investigated the effectiveness of inclusion in science instruction classrooms and determined how to support high school students with specific learning disabilities (SLD) in general education classrooms in the best way possible (Thornton et al., 2015; Woodcock &Vialle, 2010). They found some functional relations between the introduction of collaborative pre-teaching and improvement in students' performance on daily biology tests.

REVIEW OF RESEARCH LITERATURE

Until the early 2000s, students in special education programs experienced different educational experiences; in some cases, students received no help, while in others, students received access to services that helped improve their situations (Beauchamp-Pryor, 2013). This inequity in treatment was directly linked to the disparity in resources of the students' parents (Beauchamp-Pryor, 2013).

Although the mandates of federal laws are available to everyone, affluent parents more often take advantage of the services provided than low-income parents (Ong-Dean, 2009). This results in gentrification of access to the services to improve the learning environment of students. Federal and state government agencies have been aware of these inequities and have made an effort to resolve the issue. The No Child Left Behind Act (NCLB) mandated that all students, regardless of disability status, participate in standards-based assessments required by states to assess adequate yearly progress and imposed sanctions on non-performing schools (Clement, Ruebain, & Read, 2006; Krieg, 2011). This anti-discriminatory and inclusion law required that parents be involved in decision-making and advocacy for the needs and problems of their children with disabilities, especially in the support services they value, such as receiving diagnosis, ensuring educational and social inclusion, and establishing autonomy and independence in early adulthood. In addition, this educational policy mounted pressure on school administrators to decrease performance discrepancies by redirecting educational resources from groups of high-performing students to those who are under-performing (Ong-Dean, 2009).

The NCLB enforced and promoted beneficial practices and policy development for children and young people with disabilities. ESSA and IDEA also promote best practices when it comes to the educational needs of the individual student. Clements, Reubain, and Read (2006) used anti-discriminatory and inclusive approaches involving parents and children in advocacy and decision-making and identified the existence of some common needs and problems for disabled children, young adults and their families, and the supportive services that can help to meet their needs. Included are early diagnoses, providing opportunities for autonomy, ensuring educational and social inclusion, and independence throughout early adulthood, and other social services and amenities.

Despite the efforts of the NCLB Act and inclusive education policies, there are still intervening dominant social forces, such as the presence of a disability or low socioeconomic status, that hinder progress due to teacher perceptions. Vaz et al. (2015) found that teachers based their attitudes toward inclusion on the practical implementation of inclusion in real-world classroom settings, rather than a specific ideology and understanding of inclusiveness. Influencing factors include teachers' images of teaching and learning, organization and administration, approaches to policy, and individual organizational characteristics (Hulgin & Drake, 2011). For progress to be made in inclusive education, teachers' attitudes should be addressed.

In regard to student outcomes, Henninger and Gupta (2014) found that placing children with disabilities alongside their peers who are not disabled has advantages. The first advantage is that learning-disabled students have an example from which to model behaviors, which has a significant social benefit. They develop important socialization skills as they interact with their peers. Inclusion also challenges learning-disabled students academically, as they attempt to keep pace with their nondisabled peers. Students, who are not learning disabled, benefit from the ability to interact effectively with many different types of people.

However, inclusion remains controversial in the academic arena and in society in general because it is related to educational and social values, as well as to people's sense of individual worth. Not every expert agrees with the notion that learning-disabled students should be learning alongside their otherwise non-disabled counterparts, given their disadvantage (Crowson & Brandes, 2014). Opponents question its full benefit for learning-disabled students and the possible negative impact on non-learning-disabled students (Tkachyk, 2013). There are those who believe that inclusion possesses academic, social, and emotional benefits for both learning- disabled and non-learning-disabled students (Beauchamp-Pryor, 2013). This divide has provoked a nationwide debate over the wisdom of including learning-disabled students with non-learning-disabled students in the same class settings (Connor & Ferri, 2007).

Despite this ongoing debate, many schools and teachers are embracing inclusive classrooms (Beauchamp-Pryor, 2013; Vaz et al., 2015). This is a relief to many families with learning-disabled children. Education laws are necessary so that students with learning disabilities are fully included in the general education classrooms along with their non-disabled peers (Naraian, 2011; Ricketts, 2014). Inclusive education fosters participation that stems from generalized visions for promoting democratic practices within classrooms and elicits student involvement. Parents are empowered to look for the best for their children (Naraian, 2011).

REVIEW OF METHODOLOGICAL ISSUES AND LITERATURE

There are many possible ethical and methodological challenges potentially encountered in studies that involve learning-disabled students in school settings (Nind, Rix, Sheehy, & Simmons, 2014). These methodological concerns come from the school administration, parents, and the school board and surround how inclusiveness can be implemented in an orderly fashion without depriving any student of privileges or opportunities. Tkachyk (2013) found that teachers and parents question whether full inclusion will come at the expense of the individual needs of the learners. To overcome this doubt, schools and teachers need to prioritize the learning needs of all learning-disabled students when contemplating full inclusion. Laws mandate the ability to deliver instruction that meets the diverse learning needs in inclusive classrooms, meanwhile making certain that students meet grade-level expectations (Blessing, 2003).

Ricketts (2014) on the other hand, found that teachers identified lack of time, lack of support, lack of competence, lack of training opportunities, inadequate resources, and student behavioral issues as barriers to implementing differentiated instruction. Professional development and training is needed to prepare teachers and parents to successfully implement differentiated instruction. Kluth, Biklen, English-Sand, and Smukler (2007) called for considerations that promote inclusive education and for supporting families of learning-disabled students in their quest for quality education for their children. Nind et al. (2014) found a range of practical and ethical challenges that include how inclusive school cultures are recognized, how changes are affected, and how children and their experiences are handled. Issues of methodology arose when demands of navigating new classroom environments increased students' anxiety, created concerns about how students satisfied their need for belonging, and how students' perspectives regarding school influenced their attitudes toward help (Bigby, Frawley, & Ramcharan, 2014). Bigby et al. (2014) suggested that schools should facilitate school transitions for early adolescents with only mild disabilities.

In discussing the role of case studies in developing and testing theories, Cohen, Manion, and Morrison (2013) addressed the problem of generalizing from the study of a small number of cases. They reasoned that when case studies present lessons that are generalizable to new contexts and backgrounds, the results are valid. Ruzzene (2012) reasoned that when case studies are highly comparable, their external validity can be reliably and efficiently assessed, thereby enhancing their generalizability potential. In addition to challenges of generalizability, Ruzzene (2012) noted challenges of obtaining reliable data from observation. Reasoning that behavior can be influenced by multiple contextual factors, Bottema-Beutel, Lloyd, Carter, and Asmus (2014) concluded that attaining reliable estimates of observational measures could be challenging in school and classroom settings.

Research on inclusive classroom approaches may not exhaustively address the lived experience of growing up with disability, although such studies can provide valuable insight into the ways in which the "social and environmental contexts of disabled childhoods can redress the disadvantage and inequality they faced on a daily basis" (Emerson, 2012, p. 216). However, the researcher could not find studies regarding students' perceptions of their own disabilities. The literature was lacking research from students' perspectives.

The researcher conducted this study in three high schools in Michigan with its unique socio-economic history and profile. This study sought to gather teachers' perspectives on the inclusive classroom. Specifically, this study explored teachers' perspectives of inclusive classroom environments for high school seniors' learning-disabled and non-learning-disabled students in central Michigan high schools.

SYNTHESIS OF RESEARCH FINDINGS

Researchers found that inclusive approaches in teaching and learning enhance the participation and achievement of all students, including the learning-disabled (Beauchamp-Pryor, 2013; Kioko & Makoelle, 2014). Through the theories of inclusion, disability is considered a social construct that recognizes the challenges that exist within such social groups. Inclusive education is formed by a complex set of understandings. Kioko and Makoelle (2014) advocated that inter-departmental policies for best practices should not only focus exclusively on learning-disabled students but also include members of staff, students, school building staff and administrators, and parents. Additionally, Bauer et al. (2015) found that advocacy helps learning-disabled students and their families to understand their rights and choices as well as providing support in resolving their life issues. Bauer et al. (2015) argued that there is better use of available money for the support of parents of learning-disabled children than the current practice of hiring an advocate for the child.

PERSPECTIVES OF TEACHERS

Teacher perspectives of learning-disabled students impact classroom outcomes. Teachers' perceptions that students with learning disabilities cannot achieve to the same standards as non-learning-disabled students may allow personal attitudes to affect their treatment of the students. They may have a negative attitude toward the disabled population as a whole (Lisle, 2011).

Various factors influence teacher perspectives of disability and inclusive learning, but a recurring factor in the literature was teacher training. MacFarlane and Woolfson (2013) used the theory of planned behavior to explore teacher attitudes and perspectives toward children with social, emotional, and behavioral difficulties. They found that teachers who attended specialty training and acquired more knowledge developed better attitudes toward children with special needs than those who had less experience and training in this area. Similarly, Otukile-Mongwaketse and Mukhopadhyay's (2013) study found training and experience were predictors of teachers' attitudes toward children with special behavioral problems in the classroom. The study found a significant difference in attitudes between teachers in training who had performed their student teaching and those who had not (Otukile-Mongwaketse & Mukhopadhyay, 2013). The study found that preparation of the teachers was a predictor of attitudes. MacFarlane and Woolfson (2013) maintained that teachers with higher levels of preparation retained higher opinions of special-needs students than those with lower levels of training and education. This supports training and education as a significant factor in shaping the attitudes of teachers toward inclusion (MacFarlane & Woolfson, 2013).

Avissar et al. (2016) also conducted research based on the theme of teacher training and understanding of inclusion. The researchers found that teachers who had little knowledge of inclusion and children with disabilities had a negative perception of inclusion. Avissar et al. found that differences in attitude ranged from the idea of treating special-needs students the same as general population students to the attitude that these students need significant special support in order to function in the classroom.

Furthermore, Maria (2013) supported the notion that teachers' beliefs and knowledge were an important factor in their behavior within the inclusive classroom setting. However, this study differed slightly from the results of other studies because it did not measure the knowledge of the teachers, but rather what they perceived their knowledge level to be. Teachers who perceived they were more knowledgeable about inclusive education were more likely to translate this attitude into applicable practices within the classroom.

The level of support available and the responsiveness of this support network also influenced teacher attitudes toward disabled students. Rodriguez, Saldaña, and Moreno (2012) examined the variables that lead to positive attitudes among teachers of children with autism spectrum disorder. The study found the amount of support available to the teachers to be a major factor in the attitude of teachers toward children with autism spectrum disorder in the classroom. Supports may come through professional development programs, peer support, and through additional classes and workshops aimed at understanding students on the autism spectrum. Another factor was the responsiveness of the network to provide the support to them. Teachers with little support developed poor attitudes more than those with sufficient support networks. These studies highlighted the importance of training, education, and a support network in shaping the attitudes of teachers toward students with special needs in their classrooms.

Sometimes teachers' attitudes stemmed from students' abilities and behaviors. Block, Hutzler, Barak, and Klavina (2013) found self-efficacy of students with learning disabilities to be a factor in the attitudes of physical education teachers toward their ability to maintain an inclusive classroom setting. This study examined the special challenges faced by physical education teachers due to the physical limitations of special education students. Higher levels of self-efficacy predicted more positive teacher attitudes toward special-education children in the physical education setting. Malinen, Savolainen, and Xu (2012) explored the issue of self- efficacy and the inclusive classroom further. They found that teacher self-efficacy leading to teacher behaviors in the classroom could be divided into self-efficacy in using instructions, self- efficacy and collaboration, and self-efficacy in managing behavior. This research supports the need for different skills within the inclusive classroom. The teacher provides all of the necessary skills and strategies for the varying abilities in the inclusive classroom.

The adoption of inclusion has undergone a global shift regarding implementation. Inclusion continues to gain popularity around the world. However, teachers continue to have preconceived ideas and misconceptions about successful implementation in the classroom (Newton, Hunter-Johnson, Gardiner-Farquharson, & Cambridge, 2014). In addition, teachers have misconceptions about policies and procedures of inclusion and various practices in the general classroom regarding inclusion (Newton et al., 2014). The main problems that influence teacher perspectives of inclusion are lack of training, insufficient resources, lack of administrative support, pre-existing teacher attitudes, and the persistence of common misconceptions about inclusive education (Newton et al., 2014).

Throughout this section of the literature review, many studies examined the overarching theme of training and education as predictors of teacher attitudes. Teachers with a greater amount of knowledge regarding special needs children and behavior management maintained more positive attitudes than those who lacked training and skills required to teach special needs children. Another factor found in the literature review was the level of administrative support provided to teachers of inclusive classrooms.

Studies found that preconceived ideas played a role in teacher attitudes toward the inclusive classroom, but those that supported knowledge as the main predictor of teacher perspectives overshadowed these studies. Self-efficacy was also found to be important in teacher attitudes. Self-efficacy may be linked to the training and education issue, but this was not addressed in any of the literature found. Training and education of the teachers will play a significant role in the study as part of this research.

THE IMPACT OF LABELING

The connotations of labeling and the impact on learning-disabled children can be devastating. Thompson (2012) explored the psychosocial and educational aspects of labeling and stigma and concluded that they cause a negative impact on learning-disabled students. Anastasiou and Kauffman (2011) established that during the beginning of their academic careers, students were often taught what it meant to be disabled and what it would mean to be "special ed," concluding that some children formed a deviant self-identity when they were marginalized – spatially, discursively, and curricular– in the school community. Anastasiou and Kauffman (2011) suggested that by understanding these mechanics and variables, teachers could contribute in different ways to address students' unique particularities.

Job and Klassen (2012) noted that "deficit theory" is a term that describes the negative identity characteristics (labels) that teachers and school systems associate with students that they view as unprepared to benefit from normal schooling. The fragility of the mind of a young person can be damaged if not handled with care. Shifrer (2013) found that a learning disability influenced a student's personal perceptions of him or herself. Labeling a child as disabled can be injurious. Instead, educators must recognize and respect learning-disabled students' fragile emotions. Inclusion benefits students by helping them to overcome their sense of being different from others. It also increases their sense of self-efficacy and social skills. The inclusive classroom helps the labeled child to overcome the effects of labeling through "normalizing" their educational experience.

Effects of labeling and the resulting marginalization can include failure to achieve at higher levels of education. Lamberg (2012) found that students who were labeled "special needs" were less likely to enter postsecondary programs, and when they did, they were less likely to persist than their peers. This study explored teachers' perspectives of inclusive classroom environments for high school seniors' learning-disabled and non-learning-disabled students in central Michigan high schools.

IMPACT OF BULLYING

Research found that a relationship exists between learning-disabled students and the prevalence of bullying that point to a greater risk of special-needs students being victimized by their peers (Eckes & Gibbs, 2012). Teachers' perceptions of students may be affected by the actions of other students toward learning disabled students. While the teacher must remain impartial, the social and behavioral changes caused by bullying might affect the behavior of the student in the classroom, which would in turn have an effect on the perception of the teachers about the students. The effect of bullying on the classroom behavior of the students may affect the perceptions of the teacher. Various studies recognized a prevalence of bully-victimization amongst fourth through eighth graders with learning disabilities, especially students identified as nonverbal learning-disabled. Students with nonverbal learning disabilities showed greater difficulties meeting the social demands of school life as they were predisposed to peer ridiculing and rejection, given their poor interpretation of social cues (Lamberg, 2012; Maag & Katsiyannis, 2012; Rose & Monda-Amaya, 2012). Studies attempted to understand the influence of bullying on students with learning disabilities and how they cope with the experience. Huffman (2015) found that bullying experiences affected the academics of learning-disabled students and altered the way they communicated with their peers. He noted that although the students were affected in the same ways, they coped differently. Bullying is a pervasive problem in American schools that can go unnoticed by classroom teachers and building administrators (Rose & Monda-Amaya, 2012).

Hartley, Bauman, Nixon, and Davis (2015) reported that students in special education incurred physical and emotional harm as well as psychological distress because of victimization. Bullying does not always look the same. Sometimes, the outward signs of bullying are evident in the behavior of the disabled child. Other times, the child may attempt to hide the effects of bullying for fear that the perpetrator will escalate their harassment. Hartley et al. (2015) also found that adult teachers and other staff were more likely to verbally, relationally, and physically bully students in special education. The situation is such that teachers, administrators, and researchers should seek a better understanding of bullying behavior and strategies for intervening in schools and classrooms. Studies also found that special-needs students were at a greater risk of being victimized by their peers than the general student population (Hartley et al., 2015; Rose, Maag, & Katsiyannis, 2012). Given the seriousness and widespread nature of the matter, it is imperative that provisions for the security of learning-disabled students provide them protection from bullying (Lamberg, 2012).

Bullying can inflict serious physical harm on students. Bullying causes progressive damage to the nervous system, seen in symptoms such as gait disturbance, speech problems, and heart disease (Maag & Katsiyannis, 2012). According to Eckes and Gibbs (2012), learning-disabled students are harassed more than their non-disabled peers are, yet every school district is held accountable to respond to acts of harassment and can face disciplinary action for failing to do so. The Title II of the American with Disabilities Act of 1990 (ADA) and Section 504 of the Rehabilitation Act of 1973 (Section 504) prohibit school districts from discriminating against learning-disabled students. The law empowers school authorities and teachers to protect learning-disabled students in their care from any form of abuse.

Students are at their best when they are learning in socially acceptable public school environments. State and federal laws continue to guarantee the security and rights of special- needs students (Eckes & Gibbs, 2012). In addition, many times other students will provide a supportive environment for the learning-disabled students and will protect and care for them. Some students are more accepting of those that are different from them and will offer a support system for the learning-disabled student (Eckes & Gibbs, 2012).

CRITIQUE OF PREVIOUS RESEARCH ON CLASSROOM INCLUSIVENESS

Hehir and Katzman (2013) argued that since inclusive education became recommended practice for students with severe disabilities, learning-disabled students have benefitted from the richer learning environments and the natural support that general education classrooms provide. Further, literature showed the improvement of learning-disabled students when they were involved in inclusive environments as opposed to when they were in segregated classrooms. In an assessment of the social functioning of learning-disabled primary grade students, Lamberg (2012) found that learning-disabled students were initially less well liked and more frequently rejected, and maintained lower academic self-concept scores in an inclusive classroom. Learning-disabled students who participated in inclusive classes made more friends. Beauchamp-Pryor (2013) similarly found that there was progressive development when schools used inclusionary models involving all children in regular classrooms, regardless of the type or severity of any disabilities. Extending his conclusions to the tertiary levels of education, Beauchamp-Pryor (2013) concluded from his study of exclusiveness of learning-disabled students in higher education in Welsh institutions that there was a legislative and societal reawakening to change. He surmised that such trends resulted in an increased number of learning-disabled students having more access to higher education, in contrast to the 1990s era when few learning-disabled students had such opportunities. Kemp (2015) inferred that the need for renewed perception and change are less threatening for teachers in the school system, and more as part of how the system functions as schools prepare students for the future. This study explored teachers' perspectives of inclusive classroom environments for high school seniors' learning-disabled and non-learning-disabled students in central Michigan high schools.

Despite research that suggested the advantages of the inclusive classroom, other research noted tensions and challenges that exist with implementation of inclusive classrooms. School districts and families struggle to accept and include learning-disabled students in inclusive settings because of adult attitudes, teachers' unpreparedness to face the challenges of diverse student needs, and the perception that inclusive practices will happen when there is support from a strong district and building leadership (Kemp, 2015). Experts warned that a rush to the rhetoric of full inclusion of all learning-disabled students in regular education programs could be disastrous, maintaining that such movements offer only illusions of support for all students (Deku & Ackah, 2012). This study will add to the literature by studying teachers' perspectives of inclusive classroom environments for learning-disabled and non-learning-disabled for high school seniors in central Michigan.

Part of what the research suggests is that students' success in the inclusive classroom depends on the attitudes and abilities of those who create the inclusive education environment. Benefits do not accrue from classroom-related activities alone, but also from the highly individualized approaches that require collaborative teamwork with family members and peers. Vaz et al. (2015) noted that it is also important that teachers' attitudes toward inclusion are based on the practical implementation of inclusive education and their knowledge base of inclusiveness. Vaz et al. also explored behavioral descriptions of students, staff, and principals that demonstrated high commitment to inclusive education and environmental variables that provided descriptions of the cultural entities that nourished inclusiveness.

Without the right curriculum or classroom environment, inclusive classrooms may not yield benefits for learning-disabled students. Learning-disabled students continue to struggle in inclusive classrooms because the curricular objectives take precedence over the natural learning processes (Csoli, 2013). Csoli (2013) advised that students with learning disabilities should receive instruction using compensatory strategies, learning spaces that suit their needs, the freedom to make choices, honesty from educators, and the independence to maneuver their environment. Naraian (2011) argued that inclusive education research fosters participation that stems from a vision of promoting democratic practices within classrooms, which prompts the concern for eliciting student "voices." In his ethnographic study, Naraian identified "pedagogic voice" as a construct that secured participation within inclusive classrooms. School staff and families attempted to create conditions for the emergence of students' voices in the classroom setting. Obiakor et al. (2012) maintained that a curriculum could be designed, adapted, and delivered in general education classrooms in attempts to successfully promote inclusive communities. The researcher investigated teachers' perspectives of inclusive classroom environments for' learning-disabled and non-learning-disabled high school seniors in central Michigan.

Obiakor et al.'s (2012) study provoked the researchers to further explore teachers' perspectives of the benefits of inclusive education, and how their attitudes may shape, and be shaped by, their inclusive classroom experiences. Additionally, the researcher examined the roles teachers play in fostering inclusion and explored whether there were factors that inhibit improvement of learning-disabled students participating in inclusion classrooms.

SUMMARY

Empowered by IDEA and its mandate for providing the least restrictive environment for the student regarding the well-being of learning-disabled students, schools include learning- disabled students in general education classes across America. Many school systems encourage, support, and sustain inclusive learning environments (Beauchamp-Pryor, 2013; Kioko & Makoelle, 2014). Researchers maintain that society has a moral obligation to educate all children in the same classroom regardless of disabilities (Hehir & Katzman, 2013). However, inclusion remains a controversial concept for both educational and social values, as well as students' perceptions of individual worth. The federal government, school districts, parents, and students remain locked in a conflict polarizing education and families, especially at the lower educational levels. Despite controversy, the federal government mandates there should be equity and fairness in making educational resources equally accessible to every American child (Lipsky & Gartner, 2013).

Despite efforts to remedy the issues in the placement of learning-disabled students in school systems nationwide, issues such as rejection, ignorance, and discrimination toward learning-disabled students and their needs remain. Other concerns include unwarranted antagonism from teachers, classmates, parents, and building staff toward learning-disabled students (Smith et al., 2015). In the school buildings where leadership is sympathetic to the issues facing learning-disabled students and their families, a seamless establishment of inclusiveness is present. Anastasiou and Kauffman (2011) reasoned that inclusiveness of the moral universe refers to the community to which people apply moral values and rules of fairness. It is judged that moral inclusiveness involves the number of "value items focused on the welfare of non-in-group members that form a distinct region in a multidimensional scaling analysis (MDS) rather than intermixing with moral values that usually relate to the in-group" (Middleton, 2009, p. 32).

The training and knowledge of educators is important to the success of inclusive education. Principals may adopt inclusiveness policies within their schools by effectively using their knowledge of special education (Brown, 2012). Anderson (2012) reached a similar conclusion when examining the relevance of knowledge and application of professional behaviors, decisions, and ethics, and the implication of the relevance of leadership in higher education, including special education programs. Deku and Ackah (2012) advocated for a pre- service curricula that included in-service training for teachers as well as service providers. Similarly, Grant and Sleeter (2011) recognized the diversity of classrooms and recommended that in order to reach and understand students, educators must be aware of the forces of diversity: cultural, racial, ethnic, and language. Recognition of the importance of diversity among students with behavioral disorders, and the need to consider their inclusion in all levels of education should be considered. Supportive policies in K-12 education that address the needs and welfare of learning-disabled individuals and their families should be sustained (Madriaga, Hanson, Kay, & Walker, 2011). Additionally, in arguing that students with different learning abilities benefit from cooperative learning (inclusive classrooms), (Hanushek, Kain, Markman, & Rivkin, 2003; Runswick-Cole, 2011) emphasized the crucial role of parents in assisting the implementation of inclusive methods. The contributions of parents and families of learning-disabled students cannot be over-emphasized. This is crucial in reaching the educational goals of inclusion.

Overall, the literature review suggested that learning disabled students benefit from cooperative learning environments and the inclusion improves outcomes for learning disabled students. However, it was suggested that the training and knowledge of educators has a moderating effect on the outcome for students in an inclusive classroom. A majority of the researchers agreed that the inclusive classroom has an overall positive effect on outcomes for learning disabled students.

Given the efforts of the government to improve the learning environments of learning- disabled students through funding and friendly policies, this research explored teachers' perspectives of inclusive classroom environments for learning-disabled and non-learning-disabled high school seniors in central Michigan high schools.

Chapter 3
Methodology

In this study, the researcher examined teachers' perspectives of differences in learning-disabled and non-learning-disabled students' experiences in terms of social skills, behavior, and academic achievement. This study was conducted in a central Michigan public school. The study will add to the existing body of literature about teachers' perspectives of the school experiences of adolescents with learning disabilities in inclusive settings. Inclusion is a new program in the urban school system, the self-governing arm of a central Michigan public school system. Therefore, there is little evidence to support benefits of inclusion for the students socially, behaviorally, and academically.

According to Vaz et al. (2015), teacher attitudes toward inclusive classrooms are based on their own experiences with the practical implementation of inclusive education programs, as opposed to a pedagogical understanding of what inclusiveness means. Learning how these attitudes are formed and how they affect students, will help improve classroom teachers' knowledge base regarding learning-disabled students' daily lives in the inclusive classroom.

This research methodology provides insight into the perspectives of teachers regarding the impact of inclusion on learning-disabled students with the aim of improving interventions for students' learning outcomes. The researcher explored teachers' perspectives of inclusive classroom environments for learning-disabled and non-learning disabled high school seniors and gained knowledge of how students with learning disabilities can benefit from inclusive classrooms and what challenges they faced in the inclusive classroom setting. These difficulties go beyond the ability to grasp the academic classwork and extend to all areas of life (Moulya & Sirkeck, 2015). The researcher explored teachers' perspectives of inclusive classroom environments for learning-disabled and non-learning-disabled high school seniors in central Michigan. Chapter 2 demonstrated that progress has been made in improving the lives of learning-disabled students through laws, education within families, a change of mind in society, and general attitudes about learning-disabled people. The literature review suggested that although progress has been made, and circumstances have improved over time, opportunities for improvement still exist.

This chapter examines methodology for conducting the research study, rationale for the choice of design, the sample population, data collection procedures, and data analysis procedures. This chapter also provides a means for other researchers to understand the importance of the study in respect to the perspectives of teachers and the experiences of learning- disabled students in their classrooms.

RESEARCH QUESTIONS

The goal of this research was to assess teacher perspectives of how inclusion affects learning-disabled students and non-learning-disabled students socially, behaviorally, and academically in public school inclusive educational settings in central Michigan. This research was based on information discovered during the literature review that suggested that students with learning disabilities are disproportionately exposed to exclusionary discipline as compared to non- learning-disabled students (Williams et al., 2013). Exclusionary discipline can affect students' social adjustment and academic performance due to the psychological impact of separation from their peers (Williams et al., 2013). Research also found that learning-disabled students experience anxiety from perceived threats from socially dominant groups (Bustillos & Silvan-Ferrero, 2013). Other sources in the literature review highlighted the benefits of inclusion, including additional parental involvement (Engelbrecht, Oswald, Swart, Kitching, & Eloff, 2005). The researcher explored the perspectives of teachers related to the students' academics, social integration, and behavior. It also explored the teachers' perspectives on adequate training and preparedness to teach this population.

The researcher examined two research questions in this study. These questions were developed from an examination of existing literature on the perspectives of teachers in the inclusive classroom. They also evolved from the researcher's goals for the study.

What are teachers' perspectives of inclusive classroom settings and their impact on regular education students, socially, behaviorally, and academically?

What are teachers' perspectives of inclusive classroom settings and their impact on special education students, socially, behaviorally, and academically?

PURPOSE AND RATIONALE OF THE STUDY

The purpose of this study was to determine how teachers' perspectives of both learning- disabled and non-learning-disabled students in the inclusion classroom affect the academic and social success of these two groups utilizing a structured interview process. Using a structured interview methodology for this research study, the researcher examined the teachers' perspectives in hopes of answering the research questions. The in-depth interview process allowed teachers to share meaningful experiences reflecting their daily experiences in an inclusive setting. The need for this type of study arose from research conducted by Welsh (2010), who found that politics dictates school policy to parents and students. Welsh, suggested that research studies should dictate the policies about the treatment and well-being of learning-disabled students and not by political agenda.

This research study provides an in-depth knowledge base about real-world experiences of learning-disabled and non-learning-disabled students in the inclusive classroom setting, as perceived by high school inclusion teachers. This study allowed the researcher to compare the experiences of teachers of learning-disabled learners and non-learning-disabled learners in an inclusive classroom setting. One efficient way to compare experiential differences between the two categories of teachers is through in-depth interviews. In-depth interviews were conducted to better understand the perspectives of teachers on the inclusion classroom. By consulting interlocutors who directly experience the issue of interest, the researcher captured perspectives of the target audience, delved into the range of opinions on inclusion, and discerned both the origins and impact of the teachers' perspectives (Boyce & Neale, 2006; Patton, 2002).

METHODOLOGICAL DESIGN

This research used a qualitative phenomenological approach to explore teachers' perspectives of inclusive classroom environments for learning-disabled and non-learning- disabled high school seniors in central Michigan high schools. Phenomenology was chosen as a research design because of its emphasis on deriving themes from comprehensive description evoked by direct, structured inquiry. Creswell (1998) describes the thick description derived from questionnaires and dialogue as the basis for structured analysis of lived experience. In addition, phenomenology delineates methods for accounting for preconceptions, as to avoid the effects of researcher bias (Creswell, 1998). Choosing the proper research design was perhaps the most important aspect to ensure that the results of the study were both credible and transferable. Qualitative narrative research was developed in the 1970s as a response to the shortcomings of quantitative research (Lund, 2012). When the research topic calls for an in-depth examination, such as topics that examine phenomena or lived experiences, quantitative methods do not provide the type of information that is needed to draw conclusions (Gareth, 2013). The information the researcher gained in this study was intended to represent complex real-world scenarios that cannot be reduced to a single data point, and therefore a qualitative study design was appropriate. This research utilized structured interviews to gain the perspective of teachers in the inclusive classroom with both special needs and general teacher training. The research explored teachers' perspectives of inclusive classroom environments for learning-disabled and non-learning-disabled high school seniors in central Michigan. Measuring the perspectives of teachers did not lend itself to a quantitative study design, due to the type of information sought.

The phenomenological interview was an appropriate methodology for research that aimed not only to describe but to provide explanation for an observed phenomenon (Cope, 2005; Patton, 1990). This choice of methodology allowed for deep description of experiential differences among teachers of learning-disabled and non-learning-disabled classrooms while contributing theoretically to the extant literature.

Seminal works in research design theory. Baxter and Jack (2008) and Creswell (1998) suggested that researchers use case study research when the topic involves exploration of a number of different data sources. However, Giorgi (2006) cautioned against limiting a study to an individual case when analysis of numerous individuals will more accurately depict the phenomena of interest and allow for development of a common theory or structure. This is the case with the current research study and is the rationale for choosing a qualitative narrative research method. A qualitative study allows the researcher to study more than one aspect of the research phenomenon (Patton, 2002). This allows the researcher to develop a more comprehensive viewpoint of the phenomenon under study and to develop more in-depth knowledge of the topic. This was the rationale for choosing a qualitative structured interview design for this research.

One of the drawbacks of qualitative methodology is that it has been criticized as being imprecise and difficult to validate, when compared to quantitative studies (Yin, 2002). Yin (2002) believed qualitative methods could be improved so that researchers could reach a common ground between the types of research methodology. Researchers, such as Merriam (2009) and Hycner (1985), developed detailed procedures for analyzing the structured interview, with methods involving the development of thematic analysis that the researcher will analyze qualitatively. Stake (1995) devised another approach to qualitative research, an existential list approach, and suggested that researchers could modify the design slightly if they discovered that this was necessary through the course of the research study. For this research study, Hycner's methodology was the foundation of the qualitative data analysis, but Stake's perspective on modifying the methodology as needed was also considered in the research design. The seminal works of Hycner (1985), Merriam (2009), and Stake (1995) formed the theoretical foundation for the research methodology.

Defined as an arrangement of qualitative data in a systematic way in order to consolidate meaning and explanation, data coding is the optimal method of analyzing interview data (Saldaña, 2009). The researcher used in vivo coding as delineated by Saldaña (2009) to derive emerging themes from the interview transcript, and used literature to assist in interpretation of said themes. Saldaña (2009) emphasized the importance of providing appropriate questions to structure the interview, as this may shape the responses interlocutors offer and thus, the patterns in the data.

The purpose of choosing between these two types of studies is to collect data that is both useful and actionable in a timely manner (Buunk, Carmona, Bravo, Roiguez, & Peiro, 2006; Kwate & Goodman, 2015; Lindermayer et al., 2011; Saksvig et al., 2012). A cross-sectional sample was used as it allowed for description and provided a record of information present in the population at a particular point in time. Cross-sectional studies provide information that covers a shorter period of time and represents a snapshot of the sample population (Bannerjee & Chaudhury, 2010). For this study, the purpose was to develop data that could be put into action quickly to improve the lives of the students. A cross-sectional design also provides the ability to conduct the same study later to compare the two. For these reasons, the researcher chose a cross-sectional study for the study design. This type of study is divided into two cohorts that differ on the variable of interest. In this research, the variable of interest was teacher perspective, which required a qualitative approach to research, as this construct could not be reduced to a single data point.

METHODOLOGICAL CHALLENGES

Researchers encounter several challenges when conducting studies that involve learning- disabled students. The recent implementation of the inclusive classroom at the study site could influence teachers' responses to the interview questions. The inclusive classroom represents a culture that is different from the overall culture of the school system. The culture of the inclusive classroom is different because both students and teachers are expected to make accommodations and assist learning-disabled students. There is a range of reactions on how teachers recognize inclusive culture and handle disabled students in the general classroom. The transition time to the new classroom represents one of the most challenging adjustment periods for both the disabled and non-disabled student populations. This can lead to increased anxiety, concerns over creating a feeling of belonging for students, and issues of how students' perspectives affect their attitudes toward seeking help from both peers and teachers (Bigby et al., 2014). Teachers may have reported increased concerns due to this transition time.

The number of inclusive classrooms within the school system was limited, which also limited the number of teachers who volunteered for an interview (Cohen et al., 2013). This limited sample diminished the ability to transfer the information obtained in the research to other classroom situations. Each inclusive classroom was culturally unique. The student population, teacher interactions, teacher perspectives and attitudes, and teachers' previous experiences set the culture of the classroom with the population of learning-disabled students. Differences in culture in inclusive classrooms exist among school systems, but minor differences also can be found among various classroom settings. These cultural differences could have affected perspectives of the teachers as they answer the interview questions, and overall make the results not generalizable to other schools.

Qualitative research is especially vulnerable to the influence of bias (Giorgi, 2006). In qualitative research, it is imperative that the researcher avoids imposing their own viewpoints in order to bias participants or create demand effects (McMillan, 2012). Rather, the qualitative researcher must allow themes to emerge from participant responses and then use the appropriate tools and literature to interpret how those sentiments and cognitions influence behavior and academic outcomes. Hycner (1985) recommended that the researcher list all preexisting assumptions so that he or she may more effectively combat bias while analyzing data (Giorgi, 2006).

Similarly, Giorgi (2006) criticized the decontextualizing approach of several phenomenological researchers who recommend extracting only those terms relevant to the phenomena of interest. This approach does not encompass the full breadth of data, and further leads to biased analyses based on preconceptions. Giorgi also cautioned to avoid the ambiguity of undue creative interpretations of the interview. Instead, the researcher should be guided by the data (Giorgi, 2006). These protective measures help improve internal and construct validity, thus they are worth implementation

(Giorgi, 2006; Hycner, 1985).

Differences in individual classroom culture are difficult to assess using a survey technique. An in-depth interview can provide insight into classroom culture that would be missed using a questionnaire. The researcher can use observations to direct the interview to explore additional areas that were not anticipated in the development of the structured interview. The ability to make qualitative studies highly comparable increases their generalizability to a larger population (Creswell, 1998).

Curriculum design could also affect the results of the study. Curriculum differences could have a significant effect on the perspectives of the teachers in terms of the inclusive classroom. In order to eliminate the effects of the curriculum on the ability to transfer the results of the study, the researcher examined the degree of freedom teachers have in developing classroom methods and curriculum. Curriculums were standardized, eliminating this challenge.

Teacher attitudes have a significant impact on the success of the inclusive classroom. Teacher attitudes concerning learning-disabled students can affect student behavior and create challenges with integrating the student population (Lisle, 2011). A teacher may inadvertently not choose a disabled student to answer classroom questions because they do not want to embarrass the student, or the teacher may not feel that the student would know the answer. Teacher attitudes in the classroom may create a self-perpetuating cycle. A teacher with a negative attitude may inadvertently behave in such a way that creates behavioral problems with the learning-disabled student (Shifrer, 2013; Williams et al., 2013). This would then increase the negative attitude of the teacher, creating a vicious cycle that could influence the success of the inclusive classroom for all students (Cameroon, 2014).

Several factors could influence the attitudes of teachers toward learning-disabled students and the inclusive classroom setting. The amount of support and training that the teacher has regarding learning-disabled students in the classroom has an effect on the development of attitudes toward the inclusive classroom setting (Rodriguez et al., 2012). The researcher addressed factors that influence teacher perspectives in the interview process, as they had potential to significantly impact the results of the study.

These factors could affect the perspectives and attitudes of both teachers of learning- disabled students and those who teach the general classroom population. The researcher expected results of the interviews to reflect these factors in terms of teachers' perspectives of the inclusive classroom. These variables were addressed by including them in the interview questions, adding an additional dimension to the knowledge gained through the research study.

SAMPLE POPULATION SPECIFIC/ POPULATION GENERAL

The purpose of this study was to examine teacher perspectives of the performance of learning-disabled students, as compared to non-learning-disabled students, in inclusive classrooms. Qualitative studies must select participants purposefully and focus on these "information-rich" cases in depth, argued Patton (1990, p. 169). Thus, for the purpose of the study, the population included both regular classroom and special education teachers of high school senior learning-disabled and non-learning-disabled students in The Essence Educational Academy Schools. This public school system is dedicated to turning around the performance of the lowest-performing schools in the state of Michigan. They provide oversight to 15 schools, including six elementary schools and seven high schools (The Essence Educational Academy Schools of Michigan, 2017). Knowledge gained through examining the perspectives of teachers in this school system will also be applicable to the population of both regular classroom and special education teachers in high schools throughout Michigan. This form of sampling is what Patton (1990) referred to as theory-based or operational purposeful sampling, in which the researcher assesses individuals on the basis of their potential of representing the phenomena being investigated (Patton, 1990).

The researcher conducted this study using structured interview techniques to allow teachers the ability to reflect on their perspectives and to provide complete and detailed answers. Achieving an appropriate sample size for qualitative research depended on several factors. The first was the time constraints of the researcher. In qualitative research studies, it takes considerable time to gather the data and then to analyze it in a meaningful way. Heterogeneity of the sample population is another factor that influences the appropriate sample size. In a sample population where differences occur, the researcher wanted to capture a large portion of the representative qualities of the two groups. A sample size of approximately 12 teachers from each group of general and special education teachers is considered to be an appropriate sample for most studies (Baker, n.d.), but as Baker (n.d.) stated, this can change due to the availability of participants.

The researcher obtained a sample from the overall population by recruiting volunteers from the chosen school system. The researcher provided a memo to the administrative staff to make an announcement asking teachers to volunteer to participate. A total of 24 interviews were conducted over a period of 3 months, each lasting approximately 25 to 30 minutes.

The researcher then provided the 24 teacher participants with an information packet about the study and the permissions needed to participate. The packet included information about the purpose of the study and how it could help form future policy and practice regarding the inclusive classroom in the school system. A form was included for the scheduling of interviews. The researcher assured participants that the information they provide would be kept confidential and would not be accessible to anyone but the researcher.

RESEARCH INSTRUMENT

The interviews included questions that allowed the teachers to expand their thoughts. The researcher conducted a structured interview with special education teachers and general classroom teachers. This interview method, using open-ended questions, allowed for in-depth answers that provided great insight (see Chapter 4 for questions). The researcher analyzed the interview responses using coding methods for content.

RESEARCH PROCEDURES

The researcher developed research questions that examined the intended research questions for the study. Interviews were scheduled with the teachers at a time that was convenient for them. The researcher recorded the interview for transcription and coding later. The researcher followed the structured format, but allowed the teachers to add knowledge to the information provided, as they felt appropriate.

DATA ANALYSIS

The researcher transcribed the interview recordings and analyzed them using thematic coding (or delineation of significant themes and categories), according to the techniques proposed by Hycner (1985) and Merriam (2009). Merriam's data analysis system proposed that researchers organize the analytical process in three steps. The initial data preparation step involves transcribing recorded interviews (Merriam, 2009). Yin (2002) also placed an emphasis on preparation and design at the beginning of the research. Other than transcription, Hycner (1985) imparted that data preparation includes listening to the interviews as a whole and "bracketing" the data, i.e. approaching the data with openness to the meanings the interlocutors meant to communicate (Hycner, 1985).

Next, the researcher delved into the data identification step in which she developed proposed themes using the literature review and coded the interviews, while allowing for adjustment once the data was collected to account for themes that were not included in the original design (Giorgi, 2006; Merriam, 2009). Hycner (1985) identified the specifics of this step as identifying units of general meaning and deciding which of them are pertinent to the question of interest, potentially training independent coders to verify the units of meaning, reducing redundancies and grouping together units of relevant meaning.

This process led to the researcher conducting the final step, namely data manipulation. Data manipulation involves tabulating and organizing findings of the thematic analysis by creating a narrative constellation. The narrative constellation is defined by Craig (2007) as a matrix of grouped narratives that are flexibly manipulated over time. These procedures culminated in the identification of both general and unique themes for the interview data (Hycner, 1985).

The researcher expected that several research themes would develop throughout the context of coding the answers. The most likely general category was predicted to be whether the teachers' attitudes are positive or negative toward the inclusive classroom setting. Another question used in this study examined the amount of training and self-efficacy that the teachers believe they possess about their ability to effectively teach in the inclusive setting. However, additional categories developed throughout the course of the data analysis. The researcher noted these and included them in the analysis. The ability to shape the data analysis and results of the study provided a deeper understanding of the research topic than the use of only categories that are known before conducting the research study (Hycner, 1985; Stake, 1995).

LIMITATIONS OF THE RESEARCH DESIGN

This study had several limitations that affected the researcher's ability to draw conclusions based on the research methods. Confounding factors, such as existing stereotypes, and experiences with the learning-disabled population within that school district that affect the results of the research study. These confounds may affect the ability to generalize results of the research study to teachers in other school systems. It is possible that unforeseen cultural, demographic, socioeconomic, and other social factors within the school system affected the conclusions of the research.

Several limitations over which the researcher had no control might have affected the research study. One of these factors involved the past experiences of the teachers with the learning- disabled community. Teacher experience might include students with learning disabilities who were violent or aggressive. Participants may also have had pleasant experiences with disabled students. The teachers' experiences with individuals may have had an effect on their attitudes toward students with learning disabilities. These attitudes may have transferred to their perspectives on the inclusive classroom. This research examined a small sample of time but could not reflect the summary of experiences of the teachers in the study. Previous personal experience with the inclusive classroom may have had an effect on the results of the study, as it could have affected the perspectives of the teachers. Exploring this factor was beyond the scope of the study.

Dependability. Dependability affirms that the research findings are consistent and replicable. This is measured by the standard of which the research is conducted, analyzed and presented. Each process in the study should be reported in detail to enable an external researcher to repeat the inquiry and achieve similar results. This also enables researchers to understand the methods and their effectiveness (Houghton, Casey, Shaw, & Murphy, 2013). To ensure dependability, the researcher has provided details of all methods and procedure in Chapter 3. Experts in the field reviewed the interview questions to assure content was valid and dependable for answering the research questions.

Confirmability. Confirmability questions how the research findings are supported by the data collected. This is a process to establish whether the researcher has been biased during the study; this is due to the assumption that qualitative research allows the research to bring a unique perspective to the study. An external researcher can judge whether this is the case by studying the data collected during the original inquiry. To enhance the confirmability of the initial conclusion, an audit trail can be completed throughout the study to demonstrate how each decision was made (Houghton et al., 2013). To ensure confirmability and minimize the effects of bias, all preconceived notions were listed and acknowledged prior to data collection as recommended by Hycner (1985). Also, all data analysis rationales are outlined in Chapter 4 as Houghton et al. (2013) suggest.

Transferability. The transferability of the study measures the ability of the results to be applied to a differing population, setting, or context, (Burchett et al., 2012; Card, 2012). The ability to transfer the results to schools outside of the study depends on characteristics of the schools in terms of their similarity. Results of the study may be applicable to other schools that have similar socioeconomic, demographic, and setting characteristics as the schools used in the study, however care must be taken to consider the uniqueness of each situation as not to invalidate the centrality of contextual factors (Shenton, 2004).

Credibility. In quantitative research, the robustness of the study is examined in terms of the ability to repeat the same study and obtain similar results, (Burchett et al., 2012). This is referred to as the reliability of the study. However, in a qualitative research study researchers cannot repeat the interviews to determine if they would obtain the same answers. It is unlikely that sample participants would be willing to take more time to participate in the same study again. Due to difficulties in determining the reliability of a qualitative study, the measure of credibility is often used in its stead. Since the investigator is the tool in qualitative studies, it is crucial to establish the researcher's credibility via divulging relevant education, training, and connections to the topic at hand (Patton, 1999). The researcher's decades-long experience as an educator in both inclusive and non-inclusive high school classrooms, Master's in Special Education, and familiarity with the school district in which data was collected makes for a credible, informed researcher.

Credibility depends on the perspectives of the participants as to whether the instrument measured what it was intended to examine. Only the participants can determine if they felt the measure accurately represented the parameter being measured (Burchett et al., 2012), and whether the findings of the study are consistent with reality (Shenton, 2004). The researcher employed informant feedback (i.e. member checking) as an indicator for credible findings. This technique allows for the participants to examine the proposed results of the study and provide feedback on the credibility, dependability, and transferability of the study (Birt et al., 2016). This validation from the informants indicated accuracy and resonance with the lived experiences of the participants (Birt et al., 2016). Establishing credibility is crucial for ensuring trustworthiness of a given investigation (Shenton, 2004).

EXPECTED FINDINGS

The results of this study were expected to reflect the information required by the research questions and would demonstrate that differences exist in the social, behavioral, and academic performance of students in inclusive classrooms when compared with their non- learning-disabled classmates. The researcher expected differences would influence the attitudes and expectations of the teachers in terms of the performance of both special education and general classroom students. Due to differences in exposure to special education students, and differences in training, the researcher also expected that special-education teachers would have more positive attitudes toward special-education students than general classroom teachers would.

The results of the study might help to determine where changes need to be made in regards to training and professional development for teachers who have inclusive classrooms. Finding ways to close the gap between perspectives of special education and general classroom teachers regarding the inclusive setting might be beneficial to all students. The researcher expected that teachers would report that students' experience improved behavioral, social, and academic outcomes when placed in an inclusive setting. The effects of the study might have an impact on future policy regarding the inclusive classroom and its implementation.

CONFLICT OF INTEREST ASSESSMENT

The researcher was unaware of any conflicting interests that could affect the results of the study or introduce bias. The researcher had no relationship with the schools used in the study, other than as the facilitator of the interview process and research.

RESEARCHER'S POSITION

One consideration in a qualitative study is the amount of influence the researcher can have on the results of the study. Therefore, it is important to understand the position of the researcher in relation to the sample population and the study. The researcher of a qualitative study can take a position that is closer to participants than that of an observer of the phenomenon. The researcher may become close to the participants as he or she conducts the interviews, in a manner that a quantitative researcher would not. Because of this closeness and potential to become an insider, the researcher can introduce a significant amount of bias into the study. Through interactions with interviewees, the researcher can inadvertently introduce his or her own viewpoints on the subject matter, which could affect responses. In this study, the researcher – who divulged her position as a teacher in a neighboring school district – conducted in-person interviews.

The researcher in a qualitative study is both an insider and an outsider. The researcher must maintain an awareness of this position throughout the study and attempt to refrain from interaction during the coding of the interview transcriptions so that he or she does not inadvertently introduce his or her own ideas into the results provided by the respondents. In this case, the researcher retained awareness of her position and attempted to remain a conscientious, objective interviewer (Merriam, 2009).

ETHICAL ISSUES IN THE STUDY

The researcher did not expect that teachers participating in the study would experience harmful effects due to their participation. The only exception might have been slight discomfort in disclosing negative attitudes that they wished to keep hidden. For this reason, it was essential that the teachers understood their responses would be kept completely confidential and would only be viewed by the researcher during the analysis.

From an ethical standpoint, the present study had the potential to uncover that certain teachers hold implicit or explicit discriminatory attitudes toward special education students. This study may have revealed negative perspectives of which the teachers were previously unaware and this had the potential to cause discomfort. However, these revelations allow teachers to use their sentiments to improve their classroom management and attitudes toward students. The researcher expected that the discovery of these feelings would ultimately have a positive effect, in that it would encourage teachers to make changes in the way they manage their inclusive classrooms. Other than these minor psychological effects, the researcher did not expect that the study would have a significant negative impact on the study participants.

Ethical issues involving potential harm or discomfort to the teachers differ from the general ethical issues that were inherent in the study. One of these concerns was that of informed consent. As part of the interview packet, the teachers received an informed consent document that explained the purpose of the study, expectations for study participants, and any potential harm that they might incur because of participation. They signed and returned the informed consent before proceeding with the interview.

Confidentiality and assurance of privacy were also general ethical concerns of this research. The researcher assured teachers that their answers would be kept confidential and only the researcher would be able to see them. The researcher also assured them that the interview recordings and transcripts would be kept in a safe place where there was little risk of someone else being able to read them.

It might be possible that during the study the teachers will reveal confidential information about students. For example, they may use a particular example from their classroom that involves a certain student. The researcher asked teachers to refrain from revealing student names and to refer to students only by their first initials. The researcher did not have permission from the parents of the students to use their names in the study, and therefore took precautions to assure that their privacy was not breached.

SUMMARY

This section examined the rationale for choosing the research design, sample population, and research methodology used to collect data and the effects of these choices on the results of the study. The researcher formed the theoretical basis for this research methodology from seminal works in the area of qualitative research design. The researcher used an interview that contained open-ended qualitative questions to allow the teachers to reflect on their perspectives and experiences. The results were qualitative data that the researcher interpreted as appropriate to the research study.

This chapter examined several research methods that could be used to study the research questions and to explore the hypothesis. A quantitative method would not have yielded the in-depth knowledge that the researcher desired in this study. Therefore, qualitative research was the most appropriate, given the goals of the study and type of data that was used to answer the research questions. A qualitative method allowed the researcher to adjust the content analysis to reflect the participant responses. It also allowed the researcher to compare two groups of teachers in a similar fashion to a quantitative study. However, it was not limited by the constraints of a quantitative research method.

Chapter 4

Data Analysis and Results

The purpose of this qualitative research was to determine the perspectives of teachers regarding the effects of the inclusive environment on both learning-disabled and non-learning disabled students. The study explored the lived experiences of teachers in inclusive classrooms, with the aim of gaining their perspective on how inclusion affects students academically, socially, and behaviorally among general student populations and special-needs students. The study examined the following questions:

What are the teachers' perspectives of inclusive classroom settings and their impact on regular education students, socially, behaviorally, and academically?

What are teachers' perspectives of inclusive classroom settings and their impact on special education students, socially, behaviorally, and academically?

This qualitative study utilized an open-ended

interview format that was conducted by the researcher individually with the teachers, in order to gain teachers' perspectives of their experiences with learning-disabled and non-learning-disabled students in the classroom. The in-depth interview process allowed teachers to share meaningful experiences reflecting their daily experiences in an inclusive setting (Hycner, 1985). The setting for this qualitative study was a central Michigan school district.

The study drew from a population of teachers who teach learning-disabled and non-learning-disabled students in inclusive classrooms. A purposeful sample of 24, 12th grade teachers, including 12 general education and 12 special education teachers was utilized. Each participant teaches in the inclusive classroom setting of The Essence Educational Academy Schools in central Michigan. School administration developed a list of teachers that met the criteria for the study and contacted them via email to recruit them for the study. All participants were teachers in the identified schools and teach in the 12th grade inclusive classrooms.

The research questions were used as a strategy to explore the lived experiences of teachers in inclusive classrooms and to achieve the goal of the study. Data from this qualitative study was obtained by conducting individual interviews with the selected study population. The teachers consented to the auto recording of the interview sessions, which were later transcribed and coded.

DESCRIPTIVE DATA

The study procedure for this research involved interviewing the selected study population of 12 general education teachers and 12 special education teachers. Table 1 provides demographic data for study participants.

Table 1

Demographic Data for the Participants

Teacher	N=24	Percentage Breakdown
General Edu	12	50%
Special Edu	12	50%

Gender

Male	9	37%
Female	15	63%

Year Taught

1-5	1	4.2%
6-10	9	37.5%
11-20	10	41.7%
21+	4	16.6%

Figure 1 illustrates the number of years each participant has been teaching. An association was observed between perception and years of experience. Teachers with more than 11 years' experience tended to report more positive views of inclusion.

DATA COLLECTION PROCEDURE

The setting for the research was the three inclusive high school classrooms in a Michigan school district. The study procedures for this research involved conducting individual interviews with the selected study population. Meeting times were scheduled with each participant. The primary investigator interviewed each participant, recording each session on a secure device that was transcribed at a later time. The audio of each interview was transcribed in document format on a password-encrypted computer. The researcher protected against bias in the study by following procedures outlined by Hycner (1985), which advocated the acknowledgement of all pre-conceived notions prior to the start of the study.

DATA ANALYSIS AND PROCEDURES

Analysis of the data was in line with the research approach of a qualitative case study involving open-ended questions concerning the insight of participants

(Yin, 2014). The coding procedure discerned perceptions of inclusion based on common themes using ATLAS.ti software. Interview transcripts were analyzed to identify how participants describe the inclusive classroom and their perceptions in relation to regular and special education students. Initial codes were developed based on the research questions, seeking to understand the academic, behavioral, and social impacts of the inclusive classroom for regular and special education students. Open coding resulted in the development of a final coding scheme involving the impact of inclusion within general education students. The researcher coded approximately three transcripts (roughly 20%) for open coding construction. Open coding involves identification of concepts and categories and constant comparison of codes across cases (Hycner, 1985). This process was repeated to develop the final coding scheme, which was then employed to code the remaining transcripts. Social, behavioral, and academic impacts were expanded into two categories including general education impacts and special education impacts, with social, behavioral, and academic impacts for each category. Additional codes were identified during the open coding process, resulting in a final coding scheme. This included social, behavioral, and academic impacts related to how general education students perform, in addition to general positive and negative impacts and level of engagement for general education students related to the inclusive environment.

As for the impact of inclusion amongst special education students, the coding scheme likewise included social, behavioral, academic, positive, and negative effects related to the inclusive environment. The coding scheme for items involving characteristics of teachers related to the inclusive environment include specialization, experience, education/training, self-efficacy, support, resources, strategy, class environment, and benefits. An additional code was used for the perception of no impact of the inclusive environment. The definitions of each category are listed in Table 2.

Table 2

Coding Scheme

General Education Impacts	
Impacts related to the socialization, interaction with others, & general well-being of the general ed student	
Behavioral	Impacts related to how a general education student conducts oneself.
Academic	Impacts related to the student achievement & academic progress of general education students.

Positive	Positive impacts for general education students related to the inclusive environment.
Negative	Negative impacts for general education students related to the inclusive environment.
Engagement	Perceptions of general student engagement as a result of the inclusive environment.

Special Education Impacts

social	Impacts related to the socialization, interaction with others, & general well-being of the general ed students
Behavioral	Impacts related to how a special education student conducts oneself
Academic	Impacts related to the student achievement & academic progress of special education students
Positive	Positive impacts for special education students related to the inclusive environment
Negative	Negative impacts for special education students related to the inclusive environment

Engagement	Perceptions of special education student engagement as a result of the inclusive environment.

Teacher

Specialization	Refers to either general education or special education specialization of the teacher.
Experience	Refers to the experience of teaching special education students & years of experience as a teacher.
Edu/Training	Refers to education, degrees, certifications & trainings held or completed by the teacher.
Self-Efficacy	Refers to teacher's perception of ability to be effective in their role in the inclusive environment.
Support	Refers to personnel-related support including collaborating/info-sharing with other teachers & mentoring.
Resources	Refers to equipment, financial, & information to aid the learning process.
Recommendation	Refers to the teachers' stated recommendations for improvement of the inclusive environment

Strategy	Classroom strategies used by teachers to improve outcomes for general & special education students.
No Impact	Perceptions of no academic, behavioral & social impact of students compared to traditional classroom.
Class Environment	Stated descriptions or perceptions of the inclusive class environment.
Benefits	Stated perceived benefits of the inclusive classroom environment for gen & special ed students/teachers.

After completing open coding, a process of relating categorical themes to one another through critical deductions or induction known as axial coding was conducted to identify the connections made across the response codes. As a result of the axial coding process, three broad themes emerged, namely key recommendations, impact of inclusion for general education students, and impact of inclusion for special education students. Teachers perceived that inclusive environments were associated with benefits in terms of leadership and sensitivity for general education students but also negatively impacts students in terms of disruptive behavior from inclusive students. Teachers reported that inclusive environments benefit special education students due to feelings of acceptance but negatively impact them due to difficult, challenging coursework. Teachers' key recommendations included a need for additional training for teachers on co-teaching methods and special education sensitivity, a need for smaller class sizes, and a desire to return to a traditional classroom environment. Participants employed as special education teachers will be indicated with the letter "S" whereas those who are general education teachers will be indicated with "G" in the report of results that follows.

RESPONSES TO RESEARCH

Question 1: Research question 1 aimed to assess the perspectives of teachers regarding the inclusive classroom setting and the impact on regular education students, socially, behaviorally, and academically. In regards to research question 1, the following questions were asked during the interviews of general education teachers: Question 1 asked participants to describe the impact of the inclusive classroom environment in terms of academic achievement for regular education students. Answers to this question ranged from positive sentiments about social learning, leadership, and exposure to differential learning, to negative expressions concerning the difficulty catering to varying learning speeds and ability. Views on the topic varied widely, however most conceded that inclusion does not negatively impact general education students and they derive social benefits. Participant 1-G responded that, "Special education students slow down learning and take up the class instructional time for regular education students, causing the regular education students to suffer academically." Participants 2-G and 24-G responded similarly, stating that inclusion has a negative impact on the academic achievement of regular education students due to time allocated for special education students to catch up.

In contrast, participant 3 stated that inclusion could benefit all when teaching differential instruction and using hands-on-activities while participants 4-G, 7-S, 9-S, 21-G, and 22-S asserted that academic growth of regular education students is not impacted. Participant 5 stated that it depends on the demands of the teacher and how motivated the students are. Participants 8 and 19-S responded by stating inclusion helps regular education students to achieve academically by exposing them to different ways of learning, while participant 23-S mentioned the importance of exposure to different kinds of people. Participants 20-S and 5-S summarized the positive perception of inclusion academically by stating that it "helps struggling and special needs students to get needed help not only from teachers but from peers" and "peer coaching/assistance is a powerful [learning] strategy." Participants 21-G and 22-S mentioned their views that regular education students in particular are not negatively impacted by inclusion and it is easier for them to achieve than special education students.

Question 2: Asked participants to describe their perceptions of the "regular education" student's engagement in the inclusive classroom. Most participants reported that general education students are usually engaged in inclusive environments. Participants 1-G and 6-S stated that, "in general, regular education students are engaged most of the time," while participants 4, 9-S, and 19-S relayed, that regular education students display willingness to do their work and sometimes that of the special education students. Participant 5-S asserted that regular education students are somewhat but not fully engaged. Participant 7-S replied that since regular education students often serve as peer tutors, they are "distracted initially but with the proper teaching and structure, they stick to their work." Participant 24 answered that stronger students are engaged and will take pride in helping weaker students to engage. Participant 15-G reported that the general education students at their school are very often below average. Participants 2-G and 21-G emphasized the role of teachers in keeping general education students engaged, stating that, "the regular education students engage for the most part because [the teacher] makes it relevant and that the teacher has to scaffold."

Question 3: Asked participants of their overall perception of the inclusive classroom experience for regular education students. Participants generally expressed that social and diverse learning benefits are derived for general education students but the demands of inclusive classrooms put pressure on the teachers and at times leads to underachievement for general education students. Participant 5 replied that "the students are all close to the same achievement level but [inclusion] is a hindrance for regular education students' academic achievement as they wait for special education students to catch up." Participants 22-S and 23-S replied that overall inclusion is an advantage because it gives students exposure. Participant 7-S stated that it "teaches empathy, compassion, and change when things are not going well." Participant 15-G replied that regular education students "generally function just fine" and participant 19-S said that regular education students "benefit more from differentiated instructions." Participant 15-G responded that, "inclusion helps them as they see that there are better ways of doing things." Participant 9-S reported the belief that the regular education students "embrace the special education students and welcome them." Participant 21-G stated that in some instances, "it is a good thing depending on how strong the instructional teacher is and teamwork is needed." Participant 10-G contended that overall, "inclusion is more unfair because the district's personnel resources and funding are geared toward helping the special education students more." Participant 2-G opined that their sentiments on inclusion vary because sometimes they are overwhelmed by the classroom size and the amount of time spent on getting the special education students on board. Participant 22-S stated that there is not enough training for regular education teachers to be effective toward the special education students. Participant 5-S relayed that inclusion is "a hindrance for regular education students' academic achievement as they wait for special education students to catch up," while participant 6-S opined that, "there should be ability groups since the regular education students get impatient sometimes." Participant 1-G thought there was a need for a special education teacher to be present at all times to relieve some of the stress that regular education students feel. Participant 22-S stated that there is not enough training for regular education teachers to be effective toward the special education students. Participant 13-S contended that there are "zero benefits" of inclusion for both groups.

Question 4: Describe what you believe to be the main benefits for both special needs and general population students in the inclusive classroom. In sum, teachers perceived the benefits of inclusion to be social acceptance, preparation for function in society, and leadership training. Participant 9-S, 19-S, and 24-G stated that the students teach each other. Participant 3-G contended that there is no academic benefit but there may be a social benefit to inclusion. Participant 10-G stated that a benefit is "the non-isolation and socialization" of both groups of students and participant 15-G replied that inclusion helps prepare students for the real world. Participant 22-S responded by saying that, "Special education students benefit because they feel influenced. For regular education, they show compassion as requested." Participant 6-S and 7-S parroted these views, listing the benefits of inclusion as socialization and compassion and teaching of cohabitation that "mirrors society-type existence."

As for behavioral impact on general education students.

Question 5: Asked participants to describe the impact of the inclusive classroom environment in terms of behavior for regular education students. Participant 1-G stated that most times regular education students respond positively to special education students, but if the behavior of special education students gets in the way they go after each other. Participant 10-G stated that it improves their behavior due to modeling good behavior by the general education students.

Participants 5-S and 13-S asserted that there is "little to no impact" and some classes benefit greatly by having two teachers. Participant 15-G replied that there is no impact on behavior. Participant 17-G stated "the time given to special education students to catch up in their work causes the general education students to become impatient and creates more time for them to act out."

Question 6: Asked participants to describe the impact of the inclusive classroom environment in terms of socialization for special education students. Participants reported both negative and positive socialization impacts of inclusion for special education students, but the vast majority reported no negative impact. Positive impacts included the modeling of appropriate behavior by special education students, and negative impacts were described as general education students behaving worse or bullying special education students. Participant 18-S replied that behaviors are modeled from regular education students and impact positively the behavior of special education students. Participant 2-G stated that sometimes general education students want to join misbehaving special education students. Participants 5-S, 7-S, 8-S, 9-S, 13-S, 19-S, 21-G, 22-S, 23-S, and 24-G answered that there is no negative impact and the behavior is about the same. In contrast, Participant 3-G reported that generally regular education students pick on special education students because of their disabilities. Participant 24-G relayed that the reason for the lack of behavior issues amongst their students is due to the highly structured nature of their classroom.

Question 7: Asked participants about their perceptions regarding the socialization of students and acceptance among their peers for both special education and regular education students. There seemed to be two contentious viewpoints in regards to this question. Numerous participants reported that the general and special education students are accepting and compassionate to one another, whereas many reported that there is teasing and discomfort amongst the two groups. Participant 18-S responded that they "make fun of each other a lot," calling them "slow." Alternatively, participant 5-S answered that general and special education students are more compassionate as they "try to bring out the best behavior of each other." Participant 1 stated "sometimes it is difficult for regular education students to accept special education students and act nice." Participant 10-G answered that positive support from the teacher helps both groups to socialize and feel accepted by each other. Participants 12-S and 23-S stated that the students make fun of each other a lot, calling them "slow" and most special education students "stay real quiet" around the regular education students. Participant 13-S stated that special education students and regular education students form cliques amongst themselves.

In contrast, participant 3-G stated that the acceptance is very good at their school and participant 17-G said "they socialize with each other and it helps to build up the self-esteem of the special education students." Participant 19-S contended that the students "need to get along as in the real world; there are no demarcations between the 2 groups in terms of work ethics and living spaces." Participant 2-G reported that the impact depends on the student, and "they have seen some students that are withdrawn and do not feel accepted by their peers and overcompensate to get accepted whereas others don't care about being accepted but feel pressure to do things to become accepted." Participant 21-G responded by saying that the special education students "mask their disabilities and don't want to be pulled out" but the students tend to help each other overall. Thus, it is likely that social impacts vary greatly from student to student, and probably are impacted by factors such as class structure and teacher intervention in instances of bullying. As would be expected, social impacts would be more negative for students experiencing intimidation via verbal or physical threats, but such experiences can be mitigated and prevented by teachers and administrators.

Question 8: Asked participants to describe the impact

of the inclusive classroom environment in terms of socialization for regular education students. The general judgment seems to be that general education students are usually compassionate toward their disabled peers, and with the help of the teacher, both groups get along. However, sometimes sentiments of unequal ability can create divisions and lead to isolation. Participant 1-G responded that regular education students "feel that they are on a different level (academically) sometimes...and get mad and impatient with them and do not socialize as much." Participant 2-G replied that sometimes the inclusive environment is disruptive to most regular education students. Participant 10-G answered that the regular education students play the leadership role and thereby socialize well with the special education students, while participant 17-G agreed, stating that inclusion helps them to get along in school and outside the school as well. Participant 11-G reported that sometimes the inclusive students sit alone until they are in a cooperative learning environment in a laboratory setting. Participant 12-S stated that regular education students socialize with the special needs students that know how to act and participate. Participant 18-S reported that the students help each other. Participant 15-G replied that there is no impact of inclusion in terms of socialization. Participant 20-S answered that the inclusive classroom environment makes regular education students appreciate the struggles of their challenged classmates and pitch in to help. "I observe a sense of excitement and delight/fulfillment when they, the regular education students help their struggling peers achieve," participant 20-S reported.

Question 9: Asked participants to discuss what improvements they think could be made to the inclusive classroom for special needs and general education students. . In general, teachers perceived a greater need for technological and personnel resources, smaller class sizes, and adequate training for the management of inclusive classrooms. Participant 11-G responded that a common complaint for general education was a feeling that "we have little to no impact on instruction." Participant 13-S stated that it would be beneficial if there were other supports in place such as a resource room, reading, and math classes, and after school tutoring. Participant 17-G and 21-G replied that teachers should have more access to technology and to web based lessons that differentiate instructions. Participant 18-S stated that there needs to be more teachers training. Participant 2-G responded that co-teaching should be mandatory and scaffolding instructions should be provided from both teachers. Participant 7-S recommended a classroom that is heavily staffed. Participant 22-S replied, "Classrooms should not be crowded. There is a need for more workshops in differentiated instructions for regular education teachers." Participant 23-S stated that, "No improvements are needed for general education but to special education they need to take into consideration the special needs of their students." Participant 24-G responded that there are many instances where mainstream inclusion does not work while participants 9-S and 14-S agreed stating that, "they should just go back to the traditional ways, which is no inclusion." Participant 6-S asserted that every inclusive classroom should have general and special education teachers.

RESPONSES TO RESEARCH QUESTION 2

Research question 2 assessed the perspectives of teachers regarding the inclusive classroom setting and the impact on special education students, socially, behaviorally, and academically. In regards to research question 2, the following questions were asked during the interviews of general education teachers:

Question 10: Asked participants to describe the impact of the inclusive classroom environment in terms of academic achievement for special education students. In general, answers to the academic impact were not in consensus and it is likely that academic achievement depends on individual learning style and effective classroom management. Participant 1-G stated that students know about expectations and strive to do better academically. Participant 22-S agreed, stating that special education students do better in an inclusive setting. In contrast, participant 10-G stated that both groups are negatively impacted academically because of the lack of time and personnel resource to effectively teach the two groups simultaneously. Similarly, participant 19-S opined that inclusion does not have a positive impact on special needs students and participants 23-S and 24-G stated that special education students do not achieve as much.

Participant 11-G expressed a need for support from the student's resource teacher to find ways to ensure students are achieving well in his/her ability. Participants 12-S, 18-S, and 22-S reported that special education students get accommodations like extended time on tasks and modified assignments. Participants 2-G and 13-S noted that for some students it is excellent and for others it is difficult. Participant 15-G stated that special education students can achieve the same success with differentiated instruction. Participant 17-G relayed that, "Inclusion gives the special education students higher bars to reach for and achieve," revealing the commonality of the perception that the classification of special education lowers academic requirements for students. Participant 3-G responded that special education students do achieve as a result of the various accommodations in favor of special needs students as written in their IEP.

Question 11: Inquired about participants' overall perception of the inclusive classroom experience for special education students. Participant 1-G stated that sometimes the work is hard for them and they shut down. Participant 17-G relayed that it helps students to embrace the different learning styles. Participant 19-S opined that it should be looked at individually in terms of academic ability, behavior, and socially before placing students in inclusive classrooms. Participant 24-G reported that different instruction methods help students to achieve to the best of their ability. Participant 3-G asserted that having classes that are homogeneously grouped would result in more efficient learning. Participant 6-S stated that sometimes, "LD students feel left behind as teachers don't want to take time to explain things." Participant 7-S answered that, "inclusion works for special education students since it teaches them to master their next level." Participant 10-G replied that inclusion is more of a positive experience for special education students since, "they develop high self-esteem as they are not isolated." Participant 19-S stated that each student should be considered individually in terms of academic ability, behavior, and socially before placing students in inclusive classrooms. Participant 9-S responded that the regular education students "embrace the special education students and welcome them."

Question 12: Asked participants to describe their perceptions of the special education student's engagement in the inclusive classroom. Teachers generally reported that special education students experience difficulty paying attention and staying motivated. Participants 1-G and 6-S replied that special education students are not fully engaged. Participant 8-S reported that there is no difference in engagement between the two groups. Participant 7-S replied that "the children that are able to do their work, do so, but a lot of staffing is needed to keep them properly engaged." Participant 5 answered that the LD students get lost, discouraged, and are not reasonably engaged in the academic work. Participant 3-G agreed, stating that, "they don't get engaged at all and sleep most of the time." Participant 24-G responded that sometimes special education students do not want to bring attention to themselves so they are not fully engaged. Similarly, participants 2-G and 22-S stated that, "they are not engaged as the work is hard for them most of the time and they cannot complain loudly." Alternatively, participant 23-S reported that good students engage academically and participant 17-G stated that, "inclusion increases their engagement due to the fact that they are working with the higher ability students so they focus more."

Question 13: Asked participants to describe the impact of the inclusive classroom environment in terms of behavior for special education students. Participant 2-G responded that the majority of the students with IEPs get into trouble and teachers have to manipulate the lesson plan to accommodate them. Participant 17-G stated that special education students tend to have behavior issues-mainly in an attempt to cover up their inabilities. Participant 19-S asserted that, "because of the presence of the regular education students, the behavior problems sometimes diminish but if the workload is high, the behavior issues get worse." Participant 11-G agreed, reporting that, "special education students are disruptive to a class routine once class work becomes challenging." Participants 1-G and 12-S answered that emotionally impaired students "disrupt the entire flow of the classroom lessons and structure more than the rest." In contrast, participant 10-G replied that special education students tend to behave better when working with regular education students as "they do not want to be called out." Participant 22-S echoed this sentiment, stating that special education students have behavior problems but in inclusive settings, "behavior is toned down because of embarrassment."

Questions regarding recommendations for

improvements in inclusive environments yielded suggestions for improvements that were largely resource-centered.

Question 14: Asked participants to discuss what improvements they think could be made to the inclusive classroom for special needs and general education students. Participant 1-G endorsed an increase in technological tools that both groups can use and co-teaching models. Participant 10-G replied that, "there is a need for extra funding for both groups of students," while participant 12-S stated that regular education teachers need to be trained more.

Question 15: Asked participants what changes, if any, they would make to the policies and practice regarding inclusive classrooms in your school setting. Participant 1-G recommended establishing a co-teaching model where lesson plans are pre-fabricated and interpreted by both teachers. Participant 10-G endorsed redesigning inclusion classrooms to meet the needs of special education students and regular education students. Participant 11-G stated that their biggest concern is the frustration over the lack of time to collaborate with special education teachers regarding appropriate instructions and modifications that could grant further exposure to the general education curriculum. Participants 12-S, 18-S, and 19-S advocated more training for all teachers and more professional development workshops.

Participant 13 responded that, "after teachers are assigned to co-teach, there should be a set of guidelines written along with a workshop to solidify teacher roles and how it will work under the current conditions." Participant 2-G and 15-G recommended that all inclusion classrooms should have a general education teacher and an inclusion/special education teacher present at least 2–3 days per week. Participant 17-G responded that, "there should be smaller class sizes with fewer special students in them." Participant 2-G replied that policies need to be made very specific to all staff and co-teaching should be fully implemented with instructional workshops. Participant 22-S stated that, "changes should include regular education teachers taking classes for sensitivity to the special needs of the special education students." Participant 23-S replied that, "the administration should be more knowledgeable of what the inclusive setting should be and the inclusive classroom needs." Participants 3-G and 6-S endorsed "going back to the traditional classrooms of ability groupings except for a few special education students that hold their own in regular education classrooms." Thus, perceptions largely emphasized the need for more explicit and efficient training, resources, and personnel.

Question 16: Asked participants of the nature of

their school policies toward the establishment and management of inclusive classrooms. Teachers responded that their schools employed inclusion and provided guidelines and modifications for its implementation. Participants 8-S, 9-S, 21-G, 22-S, and 24-G reported that their schools mandate full inclusion. Participant 11-G advocated a need for additional focus in teacher preparation classes to help teacher candidates acquire skills for serving students with disabilities. Participant 10-G recommended mandatory differentiated instructions and accommodations as a teaching strategy in the classrooms. Participant 11-G noted a need for additional focus in teacher preparation classes to help teacher candidates acquire skills for serving students with disabilities. Participant 12-S endorsed "showing students IEPs to teachers at the beginning of the school year." Participant 13-S replied that they are working on a consistent effort to make the inclusive classroom more successful. Participant 17-G answered that, "policies include an emphasis on teacher support and differentiated instructions with the help of the special education teacher." Participant 2-G stated that students are supposed to be in inclusive settings with both teachers teaching but the co-teaching rarely happens. Participant 23-S replied by saying that, "special education needs a lot of modification for their students."

When asked what their overall perception of the inclusive classroom experience for special education students was, participant 1 replied that, "a special education teacher needs to be there at all times to take off some of the stress that regular education students feel." Participant 19-S responded it "should be looked at individually in terms of academic ability, behavior, and socially before placing students in inclusive classrooms." Participant 20-S stated that inclusion is a "great strategy, but needs more up-to date assistive technologies and adequate professional and para-professional manpower-collaborative efforts among team members." Participant 11-G stated that, "they need assistance to modify lessons at times to accommodate the inclusion student when they have a class of 32 or more." Participant 12-S stated that inclusion is not "helping the special education students." Participant 13-S responded that, "students are all close to the same achievement level in their classes and it would be beneficial if there were other support in place such as after school tutoring." Participant 6-S asserted that there should be ability groups since the regular education students get impatient sometimes. Thus, recommendations emphasized the need for smaller class sizes, co-teaching training, more efficient teaching technologies, and strategies.

Question 17: Asked participants to describe the overall

environment of the inclusive classroom in relation to student academic achievement in comparison to a traditional classroom setting. In summation, participants reported that differential teaching instruction and more diverse technology is needed in inclusive classroom environments. Participant 12-S responded that in inclusive settings, "students have accommodations and lessons are differentiated according to their academic levels unlike in the traditional classrooms." Participants 6-S, 9-S, 13-S, and 14-S stated that the overall environment is the same for both inclusive and traditional classrooms. Participant 1 responded that the classroom "helps in peer tutoring but it is a burden on the teacher to support both the regular education students and the special education ones during lessons." Participant 10-G replied that in inclusive classrooms, it is "mostly pair and share instructional strategies between lower ability students and higher ability students whereas in traditional classroom settings, it is pairing based on the same ability levels of students who can also work independently." Participant 15-G reported that inclusion requires the use of differentiated instruction and greater creativity. Participants 17-G and 18-S stated that in inclusive classrooms, "different tasks are given as opposed to traditional classrooms where the same lessons are taught and not differentiated." Participant 19-S reported that classroom sizes are larger in inclusive classrooms than in traditional classrooms. Participant 20-S stated that inclusive classroom settings are "equipped with audio-visual and graphic facilities/cues, internet and other assistive technologies, sitting arrangements, which encourage collaboration, team work, and peer support among the students."

Analysis of this experientially based data led to the derivation of consistent themes. From the inquiries regarding the effect of inclusion on general education students, it was determined that general education students receive benefits in terms of leadership and sensitivity. However, participants also felt that negative impacts of inclusion exist for general education students, namely the presence of disruptive behavior causing distraction from efficient learning. From the answers participants provided regarding the impact of inclusion on special education students, it was deduced that they receive benefits due to feelings of inclusion; however, the special education students have to contend with difficult, challenging coursework and sometimes teasing from general education students.

Key recommendations provided by participants include a need for additional training for teachers on co-teaching methods and special education sensitivity. The participants also reported the need for smaller class sizes and quite a few expressed a desire to return to the traditional classroom environment. Out of the 24 participants, 10 (42%) expressed generally positive views of inclusion, 5 (21%) expressed negative views, and 9 (36%) tended toward mixed sentiments of the impact of inclusion socially, behaviorally, and academically.

Positive views were defined as those that communicated beneficial impacts of inclusion socially, academically, or behaviorally and negative views were perceptions that relayed disadvantageous effects of inclusion. Terms such as "improve," "better," "acceptance," "teamwork," and "learn" typically indicated positive views and were coded as such, whereas terms such as "worse," "slow," impatient," "overwhelm," and "pressure" signified negative perceptions of inclusion. A code of "no impact" was signified when participants responded "none" or "no effect" to questions of impact. A general trend emerged in which the 12 educators with greater than 11 years of experience in the field tended to report more positive views of inclusion (67%), whereas those with 10 or less years of experience were more prone to report negative (50%) or mixed (40%) sentiments regarding inclusion.

SUMMARY

The sample population was obtained by recruiting volunteers through an e-mail to eligible teachers by the school principals or designee at the schools. The settings for the study were 12th grade classrooms in central Michigan high schools. The procedure for this research involved interviewing the selected study population. Data was coded using the process developed by Hycner (1985), Merriam (2009), and Stake (1995). This process allowed for the ability to collect the data and analyze it in an organized fashion, which allowed for qualitative analysis of the categories. Researchers emphasized preparation as the key to successful data interpretation using this method. The identity of research participants was kept confidential.

The researcher asked specific questions about the participants' opinions on the social, behavioral, and academic effects of inclusion on both special and regular education students. In addition, participants were encouraged to provide suggestions that would improve inclusive practices. Participants reported that they answered the open-ended questions honestly and with the knowledge they were free to decline answering any or all questions they found uncomfortable. These assurances (along with the communication of confidentiality provided to the participants) lead the researcher to reasonably assume that questions were answered honestly. The study found common themes for general education students, special education students, and key recommendations. When asked about the impact of inclusion on general education students, teachers reported that the main role of inclusion was the provision of leadership training and sensitivity for general education students. However, teachers reported that the negative impacts of inclusion include more frequent incidents of disruptive behavior causing distraction from learning. Answers provided in response to questions surrounding the effect of inclusion on special education students determined that benefits are derived from sentiments of social acceptance; however, the special education students are expected to complete more challenging coursework and sometimes endure bullying from general education students. Key suggestions provided by participants include a need for additional training for teachers on co-teaching methods and special education sensitivity. The participants also reported the necessity of smaller class sizes and a desire to return to the traditional classroom environment.

Chapter 5
Summary, Conclusions, and Recommendations

The purpose of this study was to examine the perspectives of teachers regarding social, behavioral, and academic outcomes for learning-disabled students and non-learning-disabled students in inclusive classroom settings. Extant literature cites theoretical and empirically-based benefits and drawbacks of inclusion (Beauchamp-Pryor, 2013; Hehir & Katzman, 2013), but less research is available on teacher perceptions. This research sought to give voice to those who are directly instrumental in the implementation of inclusion, since as Vaz et al. (2015) found, teachers' sentiments regarding inclusion are derived from personal experiences in the classroom rather than a specific ideology or theory. Teacher perceptions are associated with personal attitudes toward leaning-disabled and non-learning disabled students and could have consequences on student performance (Vaz et al., 2015).

Chapter 1 introduced the issue of inclusive classroom environments, delving into definitions, assumptions, the research design, and limitations of the study. Chapter 2 provided a review of background literature, while chapter 3 discussed methodology of the research study. Chapter 4 reported the results of the study, including explanations of the data analysis procedures. This chapter will interpret the results, discuss the implications of the findings, assess the relationship between those findings and prior literature, and identify limitations and directions for future research.

SUMMARY AND DISCUSSION OF RESULTS IN RELATION TO THE LITERATURE

Utilizing open-ended interviews, the current study assessed 24 teachers' perceptions of the impact of inclusion for general and special education students. Research question 1 sought to assess the perspectives of teachers regarding the inclusive classroom setting and the impact on regular education students, socially, behaviorally, and academically, while research question 2 sought to assess the impact of inclusion on special education students, socially, behaviorally, and academically. The participant pool was comprised of 12 general education teachers and 12 special education teachers. The results obtained conveyed a complicated mix of perceptions of the impact of inclusion, but general themes emerged.

Results showed teachers perceive the main benefit of inclusion for general education students is increased emotional intelligence in regards to students with disabilities. In addition, general education students were reported to receive practice with leadership and teamwork skills due to their interactions with learning-disabled students. Results showed an increase in social sensitivity. Leadership training was perceived by teachers to create positive social outcomes as a result of inclusion. This is in agreement with literature that proclaims the main advantage of inclusion to be socially based (Henninger & Gupta, 2014). Extant literature addressed this issue, finding that inclusion leads to increased focus on the salience of similarities between the two groups of students and a de-emphasis of differences (Yell et al., 2013). Students gain recognition of the challenges that exist within a social stratum, often resulting in understanding and tolerance of diverse groups (Kioko & Makoelle, 2014).

In reference to the impacts of inclusion on general education students, participants reported that special education students may disrupt a cohesive learning environment. Such distractions impede curricular progression, as reflected in statements of participants such as, "there should be ability groups since the regular education students get impatient sometimes."

However, it is apparent that inclusion does not negatively impact academics of general education students, as evidenced by the teacher participants' assertions of increased achievement of general education students in inclusive classrooms. Findings are in accordance with the research of Idol (2006), who reported that after implementation of inclusion, an Austin, Texas school district saw a significant increase in standardized test scores. This is attributable to the findings that many strategies employed for learning-disabled students provide effective instruction for students who struggle academically (Idol, 2006).

Participants reported that benefits of inclusion for special education students include feelings of social acceptance from general education students. This is in contrast with research that reported special education students experience social isolation, bullying, and rejection from peers (Wiener, 2014). Such social rejection has been linked with poor self-esteem, depression, anxiety, and poor academic achievement amongst special education students (Wiener, 2014). Participants reported that general education students are observed teasing and bullying the learning-disabled students. However, the majority of teacher participants reported sentiments of acceptance and empathy toward special education students. This is supported by research that reports fears of verbal and physical abuse of children with disabilities are often dissipated due to the rarity of occurrence and the frequency of friendships among special education and general education students occurring in inclusive classrooms (Idol, 2006).

According to participants, negative impacts of inclusion for special education students are due to the challenging coursework taught in the inclusive learning environments. Participants reported that the difficult coursework typically results either in special education students' resignation and cessation of effort to learn or special education students rising to the challenge and learning how to compete academically (Kioko & Makoelle, 2014). Exposure to a range of academic abilities allows for the emulation of peer behaviors and is linked with gaining confidence and an improved self-image among learning-disabled students (Henninger & Gupta, 2014).

Other notable findings include the frequency of communication reflecting the difficulty educators have with balancing time for attending the needs of both special education and regular education students. Learning abilities and the difference in time on academic tasks were also emphasized. This is in alignment with the assertions of Cameroon (2014) who stated that teachers are challenged when required to attend to the competing needs of general and special education students. Since special education students often require greater attention and time (Cameroon, 2014), it is the fear of many educators and parents that general education students do not receive the attention they need (Tkachyk, 2013; Wiener, 2014).

However, the interviews revealed that teachers perceive general education students to perform well academically in inclusive classrooms. Participants stated either academic growth of general education students is not impacted or inclusion helps these students achieve academically. Some participants reported that the differentiated instruction employed in inclusive classrooms help general education students to be more engaged, potentially targeting their different learning styles and increasing learning retention. Participants also reported that peer coaching also helps reinforce learning. This is in alignment with the research of Hehir and Katzman (2013) and Idol (2006) who reported, that inclusion is associated with positive academic achievement when curriculum is delivered in a way that appeals to diverse learning styles.

Out of the 24 participants, 10 (41.7%) expressed generally positive views of inclusion, five (20.8%) expressed negative views, and nine (37.5%) maintained mixed sentiments of the impact of inclusion socially, behaviorally, and academically. A theme emerged revealing educators with greater experience in the field reported more positive views of inclusion, whereas those with 10 or less years of experience were more prone to report negative or mixed sentiments regarding inclusion. This finding is interesting when considered in the context of one study, which showed that lengthier exposure to inclusion was associated with the perception of the necessity of more training with students with disabilities and a more pessimistic report of student success (Idol, 2006). Idol (2006) reported that the aforementioned participants may possess a more accurate view of the implementation of successful inclusion, and the results of the research study imply that educators with more experience may also perceive the overall necessity of inclusion.

Several participants communicated a desire to cease inclusion entirely and return to a traditional classroom. Research shows that this mindset is common. Tkachyk (2013) cautioned against the notion of inclusion, arguing that efforts to create inclusive environments should not result in the sacrifice of the needs of one group of students over another. This is a concern because studies revealed teachers and administrators may prioritize the needs of special education students over general education students (Tkachyk, 2013). Participants in the study revealed the existence of this phenomenon with statements such as, "inclusion is…unfair because the district's personnel, resources, and funding are geared toward helping the special education students more." Frustrations with the imbalances and pressure inclusion can impose when not effectively implemented may result in a desire to return to a traditional classroom. Participants perceived that funding for special education students in particular is in line with the assertions of integrated threat theory; as competition for resources become more salient, negative perceptions of the outgroup increase (Bustillos & Silvan-Ferrero, 2013). Several researchers found that concern for distribution of resources among general and special education is a significant factor in anti-inclusion sentiments among teachers, administrators, and parents (Connor & Ferri, 2007; Cook, Semmel, & Gerber, 1999; Crowson & Brandes, 2014).

However, the sentiments of other participants communicate a desire to see the successful implementation of inclusive practices. According to research, the role of administrative support and school culture impacts teacher morale. In one study, the majority of teachers interviewed reported positive perceptions of inclusion and supported the continued practice of inclusive policies, reportedly due to the support and resources supplied by administrators. Among the four schools and 125 participants, only two teachers asserted that learning-disabled students should be taught in self-contained special education classes rather than inclusive environments (Idol, 2006). This finding validates the assertions of extant literature that teachers generally oppose self-containment when considering the social and academic development of special-education students (Anderson, 2012; Cameroon, 2014; Holly, 2015).

Key recommendations and suggestions offered by the participants maintain the importance of technological resources, teacher training, need for collaboration among educators and administrators, decreased class size, and increased personnel. One participant called specifically for the collaboration between general and special education teachers regarding "appropriate instructions and modifications that could grant further exposure to the general education curriculum." Effective co-teaching has been shown to be instrumental to the success of inclusion as has professional development and training (Buysse & Hollingsworth, 2009). Effective co-teaching can not only increase student achievement but will also change teacher's perceptions. The availability of additional personnel creates a smaller student to teacher ratio, allowing for greater attentional allocation to each student and the ability to flexibly employ diverse and individualized instruction. The improvement in classroom manageability associated with co-teaching decreases stressors for educators as well, resulting in more effective instruction (Cameroon, 2014). Buysse and Hollingsworth (2009) stated that educators must be trained to be effective in serving diverse learners and differently-abled students, and professional development is essential in realizing this goal, but current standards of a quality early childhood education were developed based largely on general education students, leading to training interventions that are not properly specialized. Idol (2006) confirmed the notion that smaller classroom sizes result in more effective management of inclusive education, reporting that schools with the least number of students to teacher ratios relayed positive views of inclusion and greater student success. Overall, the research study findings are in line with seminal research on inclusion in secondary education.

This study was guided by the conceptual frameworks of integrated threat Theory (Bustillos & Silvan-Ferrero, 2013) and sociocultural theory (Cherry, 2016). Integrated threat theory explains the existence of negative perceptions of learning disabled students as a function of the desire for self-preservation in the face of a threatening social group (Bustillos & Silvan-Ferrero, 2013). Bustillos and Silvan-Ferrero (2013) argued learning-disabled students inspire a sense of threat, because of competition for resources and intergroup anxiety. A dearth of understanding and training among educators only serves to compound the implicit sense of threat symptomatic of the stigma associated with learning disabilities.

Sociocultural theory, conceived how child learning is influenced by environmental factors including culture, peers, and family socialization. Each culture endorses ways of teaching children to learn, and such learning techniques help the child navigate their environment (Roth & Lee, 2007). Both integrated threat theory and sociocultural theory explained the observed challenges that learning-disabled students contend with in the academic arena, as these students are more prone to receiving disciplinary action and experience social and academic setbacks (Ong-Dean, 2009; Williams et al., 2013).

As sociocultural theory asserts, learning-disabled children receive verbal and nonverbal communication from their social sphere of influence regarding their worth and academic ability (Cherry, 2016). Concurrently, as per integrated threat theory (Bustillos & Silvan-Ferrero, 2013), society stigmatizes individuals with disabilities due to sentiments of fear and pity for the unfamiliar and misunderstood. These processes occur synchronously, often resulting in children with disabilities who are reluctant to put forth substantial effort academically and instead misbehave (McIntosh,

Horner, Chard, Dickey, & Braun, 2008), playing out a cultural script implicitly communicated by society. However, Vaz et al. (2015) suggested that the ideology behind inclusion was less relevant than the real world, lived experiences of teachers regarding the inclusive classroom and its effects on both learning-disabled and non-learning-disabled students.

Therefore, this study contributes to the literature by revealing contemporary perceptions of inclusion and its multifaceted impact on disabled students. Findings confirm the existing literature and expose that, there exists a need for reform and continued evaluation of the effectiveness of inclusion. Finding of this study showed that teacher participants reported more positive views of inclusion the longer they were employed as educators. Results provided perspective and hope for potential improvements in inclusive practices.

LIMITATIONS

Limitations of the research study included the small sample size of 24 teacher participants from a school district in central Michigan, which detracts from the ability to generalize findings to the total population of secondary school teachers. In addition, the sample was not randomly derived which introduced bias, as does the qualitative nature of open-ended interviews (Atieno, 2009). Reliance on self-reported data leaves room for bias because of social desirability effects and characteristics introduced due to the presence of a fellow educator as the interviewer. The study design and analysis procedures do not allow for interpretations of causation in any of the reported perceptions (Atieno, 2009). Finally, the discreteness of the sample could be impacted by numerous confounding factors including teacher morale due to school-specific or district-specific pressures, leading to the observed negative reports of the impact or feasibility of inclusion.

IMPLICATIONS OF THE RESULTS FOR PRACTICE, POLICY, AND THEORY

Implication of the results of this study for practice, policy, and theory abound from both suggestions from participants and extant literature. Teacher participants communicated little to no impact on instruction and a general need for support services such as resource rooms, access to technology, more teacher training, smaller class sizes, heavily staffed classrooms, and mandatory co-teaching. The success of inclusive education is contingent on the development of cooperation and trust among educators, parents, and professionals (Walton, 2011). Such collaboration allows students to experience coherence when passing between these environments.

Appraised from a theoretical perspective, decreasing intergroup anxiety through inclusion decreases threat, and potentially leads to reduction in the amount of exclusionary discipline for learning-disabled students (Williams et al., 2013). Increasing resources such as personnel and technology may also reduce threat and improve teacher attitudes toward inclusion (Williams et al., 2013). Reducing the challenge of catering to both special education and regular education students while employing effective co-teaching practices should increase the effectiveness of inclusion (Cameroon, 2014; Casale-Giannola, 2012).

Buysse and Hollingsworth (2009) advocated the need for reform in professional development training for educators of learning-disabled students. The authors proposed a conceptual framework that emphasized who the learners are and what their unique needs are, what knowledge and skills are necessary for educators to attain and how to approach the sharpening of such professional competencies (Buysse & Hollingsworth, 2009). The authors reported the necessity of educators and associated practitioners reaching an agreement in regards to what constitutes a quality inclusive program. Identifying criteria for successful inclusion provides a future goal, as well as the development of a tool to measure the aforementioned criteria to reach state benchmarks and standards.

After conducting interviews of teachers and principals employed at schools utilizing inclusive classroom environments, Idol (2006) found that schools with the fewest learning-disabled students implement inclusion successfully. Support from administrators was predictive of this success, as every administrator was a proponent of inclusion with support for the classroom teacher. This support came specifically in the form of a special educator or teaching assistant working collaboratively to reach classroom goals. Other alternatives included supportive resource services with the resource teacher collaborating with the classroom teacher to present material that reinforced the lessons presented in the classroom curriculum. This study and others showed effective inclusion utilizes additional practitioners to address the needs of both learning-disabled and regular education students.

George (2017) advocated the use of cooperative learning techniques to increase engagement and improve test scores among all students. Utilizing interactions between students to increase their mastery of concepts work simultaneously to encourage the social advantages of inclusive practices while reinforcing learning through peer coaching and teamwork. Idol (2006) reported that in half of studied schools, teachers perceived that student attitudes toward special education students had improved as a direct result of inclusion. In addition, the majority of schools surveyed reported a significant improvement in student test scores after the implementation of inclusion using cooperative learning (Idol, 2006). Many of the same strategies that work with students who are at risk for school failure also work for certain students with disabilities. This practice was evident in several classrooms across the four schools. As schools move in this direction, it is important to monitor other students in a classroom that are benefiting from inclusion strategies, the special education consulting teacher, and the classroom teacher to develop improved strategies for disabled students.

Kioko and Makoelle (2014) suggested that including learning-disabled students in general education, instead of separating or isolating them, engenders survival instincts in the students. The equalization of opportunities requires new processes to deliver the goals of the rights of people with disabilities to remain in their communities while receiving schooling and necessary social support within the usual available structures (Tkachyk, 2013). Learning-disabled students have an inherent right to receive education in the environment least restrictive to their educational growth, and policies empirically supported to garner success. Educators who are directly instrumental in the success or failure of inclusion should consider utilizing the development of more effective inclusive techniques. Successful collaboration between educators, administrators, and support personnel is necessary for the future growth in successful inclusion.

RECOMMENDATIONS FOR FURTHER RESEARCH

Future studies should employ a random controlled experimental design in order to directly assess whether inclusion is beneficial with both groups of students academically, behaviorally, and socially. Short term experiments involving inclusion and traditional teaching environments would prove beneficial. Idol's (2006) research utilized a quantitative method assessing similar research questions. Teacher participants rated themselves on the possession of skills including adaptation to instruction, modification of curriculum, student discipline and classroom management. The researcher derived numeric scores and percentages of teachers who reported a need for more training with disabled individuals or who endorsed continuing inclusive practices. Such questionnaire data may prove useful in future studies. Further research may look more closely at the school's culture, which may impact both teacher and school administrator's perception toward inclusion. Another possibility is to look at the views of school based administrators. School leaders also may impact the perspectives of teachers and staff.

Conclusion

In conclusion, participants in the study expressed similar sentiments with findings in extant literature (Beauchamp-Pryor, 2013; Hehir & Katzman, 2013). When queried on the impact of inclusion on general education students, teachers shared that inclusion was beneficial in its provisions of leadership training and sensitivity for general education students. Participants shared that negative impacts of inclusion such as incidents of disruptive behavior occasionally detract from learning. Responses regarding the effect of inclusion on special education students revealed benefits of social acceptance but high academic standards placed on special education students and incidents of bullying make inclusion a challenge. Key recommendations included a need for additional training on co-teaching methods and special education sensitivity. Participants expressed the need for smaller class sizes and a desire to return to the traditional classroom environment.

The importance of this study is in the provision of timely information for teachers, administrators, parents, and students regarding teachers' perspectives on the inclusion educational setting for the learning-disabled population. This study also provided insight on the effects of placement in an inclusive setting on learning-disabled students and general education students. In addition, the information pertaining to teacher perceptions in inclusive classrooms will assist administrators and educational policy makers in providing effective professional development. This study also revealed the importance of co-teaching, including support personnel to ease the integration of inclusive classrooms for both students and teachers. With the help of support staff and increased training on behavioral management and differential instruction, teachers will become better equipped for successful management of inclusive classrooms. Such changes to classroom policy will lead to strides in bridging the achievement gap between learning-disabled and general education students.

REFERENCES

Alquraini, T., & Gut, D. (2012). Critical components of successful inclusion of students with severe disabilities: Literature review. International Journal of Special Education, 27(1), 42–59.

Anastasiou, D., & Kauffman, J. M. (2011). A social constructionist approach to disability: Implications for special education. Exceptional Children, 77(3), 367–384.

Anderson, E. K. (2012). The experiences of teachers serving learning-learning-disabled students in special education: A phenomenological study (Doctoral dissertation). Retrieved from ProQuest Dissertation & Theses database. (UMI No. 1019808396)

Atieno, O. P. (2009). An analysis of the strengths and limitation of qualitative and quantitative research paradigms. Problems of Education in the 21st Century, 13(1), 13–38.

Avissar, G., Lict, P., & Vogel, G. (2016). Equality? Inclusion? Do they go hand-in-hand? Policy makers' perspectives of inclusion of pupils with special needs: An exploratory study. Universal Journal of Educational Research, 4(5), 973–979.

Baker, S. (n.d.). How many qualitative interviews

is enough? National Center for Research Methods Review Paper. Retrieved from http://eprints.ncrm.ac.uk/2273/4/how_many_interviews.pdf

Bannerjee, A., & Chaudhury, S. (2010). Statistics without tears: Populations and samples. Industrial Psychiatry Journal, 19(1), 60–85.

Bauer, A., Wistow, G., Dixon, J., & Knapp, M. (2015). Investing in advocacy for parents with learning disabilities: What is the economic argument? British Journal of Learning Disabilities, 43(1), 66–74.

Baxter, P., & Jack, S. (2008). Qualitative case study methodology: Study design and implementation for novice researchers. The Qualitative Report, 13(4), 544–559. Retrieved from http://www.nova.edu/ssss/QR/QR13-4/baxter.pdf

Beauchamp-Pryor, K. (2013). Learning-disabled students in Welsh higher education: A framework for equality. Studies in Inclusive Education. The Netherlands: Sense Publishers.

Bigby, C., Frawley, P., & Ramcharan, P. (2014). Conceptualizing inclusive research with people with intellectual disability. Journal of Applied Research in Intellectual Disabilities, 27(1), 3–12.

Birt, L., Scott, S., Cavers, D., Campbell, C., & Walter, F. (2016). Member checking: A tool to enhance trustworthiness or merely a nod to validation?. Qualitative Health Research, 26(13), 1802-1811.

Blessing, C. (2003). Setting the standard for inclusion in the classroom: Transitions. Retrieved from http://digitalcommons.ilr.cornell.edu/cgi/viewcontent.cgi?article=1110&context=edicollect

Block, M., Hutzler, Y., Barak, S., & Klavina, A. (2013). Creation and validation of the self- efficacy instrument for physical education teacher education majors towards inclusion. Adapted Physical Activity Quarterly, 29, 184–205.

Bottema-Beutel, K., Lloyd, B., Carter, E. W., & Asmus, J. A. (2014). Generalizability and decision studies to inform observational and experimental research in classroom settings. American Journal on Intellectual and Developmental Disabilities, 119(6), 589.

Boyce, C., & Neale, P. (2006). Conducting in-depth interviews: A guide for designing and conducting in-depth interviews for evaluation input. Pathfinder International, 2, 1–12.

Brown, H. (2012). Not only a crime but a tragedy […] exploring the murder of adults with disability by their parents. The Journal of Adult Protection, 14(1), 6–21.

Burchett, H. E., Mayhew, S. H., Lavis, J. N., & Dobrow, M. J. (2013). When can research from one setting be useful in another? Understanding perceptions of the applicability and transferability of research. Health promotion international, 28(3), 418–430.

Bustillos, A., & Silvan-Ferrero, M. P. (2013). Attitudes towards peers with physical disabilities at high school: Applying the integrated threat theory. Rehabilitation Counseling Bulletin, 56(2), 108–119.

Buunk, A. P., Carmona, C., Bravo, M. J., Roiguez, & Peiro, J. M. (2006). Do social comparison and coping styles play a role in the development of burnout? Cross-sectional and longitudinal findings. Journal of Occupational and Organizational Psychology, 79(1), 85–99.

Buysee, V., & Hollingsworth, H. L. (2009). Program quality and early childhood inclusion: Recommendations for professional development. Topics in Early Childhood Special Education, 29(2), 119–128.

Cameroon, D. L. (2014). An examination of teacher-student interactions in inclusive classrooms: Teacher interviews and classroom observations. Journal of Research in Special Educational Needs, 14(4), 264–273.

Card, N. A. (2012). Applied meta-analysis for social science research. New York, NY: Guilford Press.

Chen, C. P., & Chan, J. (2014). Career guidance for

learning-disabled youth. International Journal for Educational and Vocational Guidance, 14(3), 275–291.

Cherry, K. (2016, October 3). What is sociocultural theory? Very well. Retrieved from https://www.verywell.com/what-is-sociocultural-theory-2795088

Clements, L., Reubain, D., & Read, J. (2006). Disabled children and the law: Research and good practice (2nd ed.). Philadelphia, PA: Jessica Kingsley Publishers, Inc.

Cohen, L., Manion, L., & Morrison, K. (2013). Research methods in education. New York, NY: Routledge.

Connor, D. J., & Ferri, B. A. (2007). The conflict within Resistance to inclusion and other paradoxes in special education. Disability & Society, 22(1), 63–77.

Cook, B. G., & Cameron, D. L. (2010). Inclusive teachers' concern and rejection toward their students: Investigating the validity of ratings and comparing student groups. Remedial and Special Education, 31(2), 67–76.

Cook, B. G., Semmel, M. L., & Gerber, M. M. (1999). Attitudes of principals and special education teachers toward the inclusion of students with mild disabilities: Critical differences of opinion. Remedial and Special Education, 20(4), 199–207.

Cope, J. (2005). Researching entrepreneurship

through phenomenological inquiry: Philosophical and methodological issues. International Small Business Journal, 23(2), 163–189.

Craig, C. J. (2007). Story constellations: A narrative approach to contextualizing teachers' knowledge of school reform. Teaching and Teacher Education, 23(2), 173–188.

Creswell, J. (1998). Research design: Qualitative, quantitative, and mixed methods approaches (2nd ed.). Thousand Oaks, CA: SAGE Publications.

Crowson, H. M., & Brandes, J. A. (2014). Predicting pre-service teachers' opposition to inclusion of learning-disabled students: A path analysis study. Social Psychology of Education, 17(1), 161–178.

Csoli, K. (2013). Natural learning and learning disabilities: What I've learned as the parent of a 2-year old. Journal of Unschooling and Alternative Learning, 7(14), 92–104.

Deku, P., & Ackah, F. R., Jr. (2012). Teachers' conceptualization of inclusive education in Ghana. Ife Psychologia, 20(1), 152.

Dudley-Marling, C., & Burns, M. (2014). Two perspectives on inclusion in the United States. Global Education Review, 1(1), 14–31. Retrieved from http://files.eric.ed.gov/fulltext/EJ1055208.pdf

Eckes, S., & Gibbs, J. (2012). The legal aspects of bullying and harassment of students with disabilities: School leaders' legal obligation. Journal of School Leadership, 22(6), 1065.

Ellis, T. J., & Levy, Y. (2009). Towards a guide for novice researchers on research methodology: Review and proposed methods. Issues in Informing Science and Information Technology, 6(1), 323–337.

Emerson, E. (2012). Understanding disabled childhoods: What can we learn from population-based studies? Children & Society, 26(3), 214–222.

Engelbrecht, P., Oswald, M., Swart, E., Kitching, A., & Eloff, I. (2005). Parents' experiences of their rights in the implementation of inclusive education in South Africa. School Psychology International, 26(4), 459–477.

Gareth, G. (2013). Demystifying mixed methods research design. Mevlana International Journal of Education, 3(2), 112–122.

Gasteiger-Klicpera, B., Klicpera, C., Gebhardt, M., & Schwab, S. (2013). Attitudes and experiences of parents regarding inclusive and special school education for children with learning and intellectual disabilities. International Journal of Inclusive Education, 17(7), 663–681.

George, R. L. (2017). Teacher perception of cooperative learning strategies impacting English learner engagement and academic performance levels (Doctoral dissertation). Retrieved from http://commons.cu-portland.edu/edudissertations/26

Giorgi, A. (2006). Concerning variations in the application of the phenomenological method. The Humanistic Psychologist, 34(4), 305.

Grant, C. A., & Sleeter, C. E. (2011). Doing multicultural education for achievement and equity. New York, NY: Routledge.

Hanushek, E. A., Kain, J. F., Markman, J. M., & Rivkin, S. G. (2003). Does peer ability affect student achievement? Journal of applied econometrics, 18(5), 527–544.

Hartley, M. T., Bauman, S., Nixon, C, L., & Davis, S. (2015). Comparative study of bullying victimization among students in general and special education. Exceptional Children, 81(2), 176–193.

Hehir, T., & Katzman, L. (2013). Effective inclusive schools: Designing successful schoolwide programs. Hoboken, NJ: Jossey-Bass.

Henninger, W., & Gupta, S. (2014). How do children benefit from inclusion? Baltimore, MD: Brookes Publishing.

Holley, J. (2015). Teacher attitudes: An analysis of middle school teachers' attitudes towards inclusion (Doctoral dissertation). Retrieved from http://mds.marshall.edu/cgi/viewcontent.cgi?article=1973&context=etd

Houghton, C., Casey, D., Shaw, D., & Murphy, K. (2013). Rigour in qualitative case-study research. Nurse researcher, 20(4), 12-17.

Huffman, A. W. (2015). Emotional consequences of learning-learning-disabled students who have been bullied at the middle school level. Sciences, 63(9), 382–391.

Hulgin, K. M., & Drake, B. M. (2011). Inclusive education and the No Child Left behind Act: Resisting entrenchment. International Journal of Inclusive Education, 15(4), 389.

Hycner, R. (1985). Some guidelines for the phenomenological analysis of interview data. Human Studies, 8, 279–303.

Idol, L. (2006). Toward inclusion of special education students in general education: A program evaluation of eight schools. Remedial and Special Education, 27(2), 77–94.

Job, J. M., & Klassen, R. M. (2012). Predicting performance on academic and non-academic tasks: A comparison of adolescents with and without learning disabilities. Contemporary Educational Psychology, 37(2), 162–169.

Karande, S., & Kuril, S. (2011). Impact of parenting practices on parent-child relationships in children with specific learning disability. Journal of Postgraduate Medicine, 57(1), 20–30.

Katsiyannis, A., Yell, M. L., & Bradley, R. (2001). Reflections on the 25th anniversary of the Individuals with Disabilities Education Act. Remedial and Special Education, 22(6), 324–334.

Kemp, C. W. (2015). Inclusive education for preschool - 12th-grade students with low incidence disability: A case study of state leaders' perception (Doctoral dissertation). Retrieved from http://digitalcommons.liberty.edu/doctoral/1124

Keogh, B. K. (2007). Celebrating PL 94–142: The Education of All Handicapped Children Act of 1975. Issues in Teacher Education, 16(2), 65–69.

Kioko, V. K., & Makoelle, T. S. (2014). Inclusion in higher education: Learning experiences of learning-disabled students at Winchester University. International Education Studies, 7(6), 106.

Kluth, P., Biklen, D., English-Sand, P., & Smukler, D. (2007). Going away to school: Stories of families who move to seek inclusive educational experiences for their children with disabilities. Journal of Disability Policy Studies, 18(1), 43–56.

Krieg, J. M. (2011). Which students are left behind? The racial impacts of the No Child Left Behind Act. Economics of Education Review, 30(4), 654–664.

Kwate, N. O. A., & Goodman, M. S. (2015). Cross-sectional and longitudinal effects of racism on mental health among residents of Black neighborhoods in New York. American Journal of Public Health, 105(4), 711–718.

Lamberg, C. D. (2012). A study of perceived admission and achievement barriers of learning-learning-disabled students in postsecondary institutions (Doctoral dissertation). Retrieved from ProQuest Dissertation & Theses database. (UMI No 3570361)

Lindenmayer, D. B., Wood, J., McBurney, L., Michael, D., Crane, M., MacGregor, C., ... & Banks, S. C. (2011). Cross-sectional vs. longitudinal research: a case study of trees with hollows and marsupials in Australian forests. Ecological Monographs, 81(4), 557–580.

Lipsky, D. K., & Gartner, A. (2013). Inclusive education: A requirement of a democratic society. World Yearbook of Education 1999: Inclusive Education. New York, NY: Routledge.

Lisle, K. (2011). Identifying the negative stigma

associated with having a learning disability (Honor theses). Bucknell University.

Lund, T. (2012). Combining qualitative and quantitative approaches: Some arguments for mixed methods research. Scandinavian Journal of Educational Research, 56(2), 155–165. doi:10.1080/00313831.2011.568674

Maag, J. W., & Katsiyannis, A. (2012). Bullying and learning-disabled students: Legal and practice consideration. Behavioral Disorders, 37(2), 78–86.

MacFarlane, K., & Woolfson, L. (2013). Inclusion of children with social, emotional and behavioral difficulties in mainstream schools: An application of the theory of planned behavior. Teaching and Teacher Education, 29, 46–52.

Madriaga, M., Hanson, K., Kay, H., & Walker, A. (2011). Marking-out normalcy and disability in higher education. British Journal of Sociology of Education, 32(6), 901–920.

Malinen, O. P., Savolainen, H., & Xu, J. (2012). Beijing in-service teachers' self-efficacy and attitudes towards inclusive education. Teaching and Teacher Education, 28(4), 526–534.

Maria, U. (2013). Teachers' perception, knowledge and behavior in inclusive education. Procedia-social and

Behavior Sciences, 84, 1237–1241.

Mariga, L., & McConkey, R. (2014). Inclusive education in low-income countries, Cape Town: Atlas Alliance and Disability Innovations Africa. Retrieved from http://www.eenet.org.uk/resources/docs/Inclusive_Education_in_Low_Income_Countries.pdf

McIntosh, K., Horner, R. H., Chard, D. J., Dickey, C. R., & Braun, D. H. (2008). Reading skills and function of problem behavior in typical school settings. The Journal of Special Education, 42(3), 131–147.

McMillan, J. H. (2012). Educational research: Fundamentals for the consumer (6th ed.). Boston, MA: Pearson.

Merriam, S. B. (2009). Qualitative research: A guide to design and implementation. San Francisco, CA: Jossey-Bass.

Michailakis, D., & Reich, W. (2009). Dilemmas of inclusive education. European Journal of Disability Research, 3(1), 24–44.

Middleton, C. R. (2009). Roosevelt University and inclusiveness in American higher education. Journal of Diversity in Higher Education, 2(1), 30–34.

Moulya, R., & Sirkeck, P. (2015). Perceived parental practices and quality of life of children with learning disabilities. The International Journal of Indian Psychology, 2(3), 83–91.

Naraian, S. (2011). Pedagogic voicing: The struggle for participation in inclusive classroom. Anthropology & Education Quarterly, 42(3), 245–262.

Newton, N., Hunter-Johnson, Y., Gardiner-Farquharson, B., & Cambridge, J. (2014). Bahamian teachers' perspectives of inclusion as a foundational platform for adult education programs. International Journal of Special Education, 29(3), 26–37.

Nind, M., Rix, J., Sheehy, K., & Simmons, K. (Eds.). (2014). Ethics and research in inclusive education: Values into practice. New York, NY: Routledge.

Obiakor, F. E., Harris, M., Mutua, K., Rotatori, A., & Algozzine, B. (2012). Making inclusion work in general education classrooms. Education and Treatment of Children, 35(3), 477–490.

Ong-Dean, C. (2009). Distinguishing disability: Parents, privilege, and special education. Chicago, IL: University of Chicago Press.

Otukile-Mongwaketse, M., & Mukhopadhyay, S. (2013). Botswana PGDE student teachers' attitude towards inclusive education: Implication for teacher education. Turkish Journal of Teacher Education, 2(1), 36–46.

Patton, M. Q. (1990). Qualitative evaluation and research methods. Thousand Oaks, CA: Sage.

Patton, M. Q. (2002). Two decades of developments in qualitative inquiry: A personal, experiential perspective. Qualitative social work, 1(3), 261–283.

Peacock Hill Working Group. (2017). Problems and promises in special education and related services for children and youth with emotional or behavioral disorders. Behavioral Disorders, 16(4), 299–313.

Ricketts, M. A. (2014). The lived experiences of teachers in implementing differentiated instruction in the inclusive classroom. (Doctoral dissertation). Retrieved from ProQuest Dissertation & Theses database. (UMI No 3645551).

Ridnouer, K. (2011). Everyday engagement: Making solutions and parents your partners in learning. Alexandria, VA: ASCD.

Rodriguez, I., Saldaña, D., & Moreno, E. (2012). Support, inclusion, and special education teacher's attitudes toward the education of students with autism spectrum disorders. Autism research and treatment. Retrieved from https://www.hindawi.com/journals/aurt/2012/259468/

Rose, C. A., & Monda-Amaya, L. E. (2012). Bullying and victimization among students with disabilities:

Effective strategies for classroom teachers. Intervention in School and Clinic, 48(2), 99–107.

Roth, W. M., & Lee, Y. J. (2007). Vygotsky's neglected legacy: Cultural historical activity theory. Review of Educational Research, 77(2), 186–232.

Runswick-Cole, K. (2011). Time to end the bias towards inclusive education? British Journal of Special Education, 38(3), 112–119.

Ruzzene, A. (2012). Drawing lessons from case studies by enhancing comparability. Philosophy of the Social Sciences, 42(1), 99–120. doi:10.1155/2012/259468

Saksvig, B., Webber, L., Elder, J., Evenson, K., Dowda, M., & Chae, S. (2012). A cross-sectional and longitudinal study of travel by walking before and after school among eighth-grade girls. Journal of Adolescent Health, 51(6), 608–614.

Saldaña, J. (2009). An introduction to codes and coding. The coding manual for qualitative researchers, 1–31.

Schalock, R. L., Borthwick-Duffy, S. A., Bradley, V. J., Buntinx, W. H., Coulter, D. L., Craig, E. M., & Shogren, K. A. (2010). Intellectual disability: Definition, classification, and systems of supports. Washington, DC: American Association on Intellectual and Developmental Disabilities.

Shenton, A. K. (2004). Strategies for ensuring trustworthiness in qualitative research projects. Education for information, 22(2), 63-75.

Shifrer, D. (2013). Stigma of a label educational expectations for high school students labeled with learning disabilities. Journal of Health and Social Behavior, 54(4), 462–480.

Smith, T. E., Polloway, E. A., Patton, J. R., Dowdy, C. A., & Doughty, T. T. (2015). Teaching students with special needs in inclusive settings. Columbus, OH: Pearson.

Stake, R. E. (1995). The art of case study research. Thousand Oaks, CA: SAGE Publications.

Summer, C. (2011). Teaching students with disability. Retrieved from http://www.dsp.berkeley.edu/teachstudentswithdisab

The Essence Educational Academy Schools of Michigan. (2017). Schools. Retrieved from http://icansoar.org/schools/

Thompson, M. M. (2012). Labeling and self-esteem: Does labeling exceptional students impact their self-esteem? Support for Learning, 27(4), 158–165.

Thornton, A., McKissick, B. R., Spooner, F., Lo, Y., & Anderson, A. L. (2015). Effects of collaborative teaching on science performance of high school students with specific learning disabilities. Education & Treatment of Children, 38(3), 277.

Tkachyk, R. E. (2013). Questioning secondary inclusive education: Are inclusive classrooms always best for students? Interchange, 44(1), 15–24.

U.S. Department of Education, National Center for Education Statistics. (2016). Digest of education statistics, 2014. Retrieved from http://nces.ed.gov/pubs2016/2016006.pdf

Vaz, S., Wilson, N., Falkmer, M., Sim, A., Scott, M., & Cordier, R. et al. (2015). Factors associated with primary school teachers' attitudes towards the inclusion of learning-disabled students. PloS One, 10(8).

Vorhaus, J. S. (2014). Philosophy and profound disability: Learning from experience. Disability & Society, 29(4), 611–623.

Vygotsky, L. S. (1978). Mind in society. Cambridge, MA: Harvard University Press.

Walton, E. (2011). Getting inclusion right in South Africa. Intervention in School and Clinic, 46(4), 240–245.

Welsh, C. R. (2010). A learning paradox: Students who are gifted and learning-disabled. Retrieved from https://www.teachervision.com/special-needs/gifted-learning-disabled-puzzling-paradox

Wiener, J. (2014). Bridging the cultural gap. Perspectives on Language and Literacy, 40(4), 39. Retrieved from http://www.onlinedigeditions.com/article/Bridging+the+Cultural+Gap%3A+Communication+with+Families+of+Culturally+andLinguistically+Diverse+Students+with+Learning+Difficulties/1840778/0/article.html

Williams, J. L., Pazey, B., Shelby, L., & Yates, J. R. (2013). The enemy among us: Do school administrators perceive learning-disabled students as a threat? NASSP Bulletin, 97(2), 139–165.

Woodcock, S., & Vialle, W. (2010). The potential to learn: Pre-service teachers proposed use of instructional strategies for students with a learning disability. Contemporary Issues in Education Research, 3(10), 27.

Wright, T., & Conley, H. (2011). Gower handbook of discrimination at work. Burlington, VT: Gower Publishing Company.

Yell, M. L., Conroy, T., Katsiyannis, A., & Conroy, T. (2013). Individualized education programs and special education programming for learning-disabled students in urban schools. Fordham Urban Law Journal, 41(2),

669.

Yettick, H., Baker, R., Wickersham, M., & Hupfeld, K. (2014). Rural districts left behind? Rural districts and the challenges of administering the elementary and secondary education act. Journal of Research in Rural Education, 29(13), 1.

Yin, R. K. (2002). Case study research: Design and methods. Thousand Oaks, CA: SAGE Publications.

www.ingramcontent.com/pod-product-compliance
Lightning Source LLC
Chambersburg PA
CBHW070553160426
43199CB00014B/2484